The Living Word

Inner Land

A Guide into the Heart of the Gospel

■ ▢ ▢ ▢ ▢ **The Inner Life**
The Inner Life
The Heart
Soul and Spirit

▢ ■ ▢ ▢ ▢ **The Conscience**
The Conscience and Its Witness
The Conscience and Its Restoration

▢ ▢ ■ ▢ ▢ **Experiencing God**
The Experience of God
The Peace of God

▢ ▢ ▢ ■ ▢ **Fire and Spirit**
Light and Fire
The Holy Spirit

▢ ▢ ▢ ▢ ■ **The Living Word**

Volume 5

The Living Word

Eberhard Arnold

PLOUGH PUBLISHING HOUSE

Published by Plough Publishing House
Walden, New York, USA
Robertsbridge, East Sussex, UK
Elsmore, NSW, Australia

Plough is the publishing house of the Bruderhof, an international community of families and singles seeking to follow Jesus together. Members of the Bruderhof are committed to a way of radical discipleship in the spirit of the Sermon on the Mount. Inspired by the first church in Jerusalem (Acts 2 and 4), they renounce private property and share everything in common in a life of nonviolence, justice, and service to neighbors near and far. To learn more about the Bruderhof's faith, history, and daily life, see Bruderhof.com.

Translated from the 1936 edition of *Innen Land: Ein Wegweiser in die Seele der Bibel und in den Kampf um die Wirklichkeit* (Buchverlag des Almbruderhof e. V.). This edition is based on the 1975 English edition translated by Winifred Hildel and Miriam Potts. Cover image: *Sky Burst* (oil on canvas) by Erin Hanson, copyright © Erin Hanson. Used with permission.

A catalog record for this book is available from the British Library. Library of Congress Cataloging-in-Publication Data pending.

Printed in the United States

Contents

Preface　*vii*

Introduction by J. Heinrich Arnold　*xi*

The Living Word　1

Preface

Born to an academic family in the Prussian city of
Königsberg, Eberhard Arnold (1883–1935) received a
doctorate in philosophy and became a sought-after
writer and speaker in Germany. Yet like thousands
of other young Europeans in the turbulent years
following World War I, he and his wife, Emmy,
were disillusioned by the failure of the establish-
ment – especially the churches – to provide answers
to the problems facing society.

In 1920, out of a desire to put into practice the
teachings of Jesus, the Arnolds turned their backs
on the privileges of middle-class life in Berlin and
moved to the village of Sannerz with their five young
children. There, with a handful of others, they started
an intentional community on the basis of the Sermon
on the Mount, drawing inspiration from the early
Christians and the sixteenth-century Anabaptists.
The community, which supported itself by agricul-
ture and publishing, attracted thousands of visitors
and eventually grew into the international movement
known as the Bruderhof.

Eberhard Arnold's magnum opus, *Inner Land*, absorbed his energies off and on for most of his adult life. Begun in the months before World War I broke out, the first version of the book was published in 1914 as a patriotic pamphlet for German soldiers titled *War: A Call to Inwardness*. The first version to carry the title *Inner Land* appeared after the war in 1918; Arnold had extensively revised the text in light of his embrace of Christian pacifism. In 1932 Arnold began a new edit, reflecting the influence of religious socialism and his immersion in the writings of the sixteenth-century Radical Reformation, as well as his experiences living in the Sannerz community. Arnold continued to rework the book during the following three years, as he and the community became targets of increasing harassment as opponents of Nazism. The final text, on which this translation is based, was published in 1936. Arnold had died one year earlier as the result of a failed surgery, before completing this final chapter. Up to page 56 of this volume he had declared the manuscript ready for print. The text was completed after his death, based on talks he had held in October 1933. The conclusion was taken from the 1923 edition.

This final version of *Inner Land* was not explicitly critical of the Nazi regime. Instead, it attacked the spirits that fed German society's support for Nazism: racism and bigotry, nationalistic fervor, hatred of political enemies, a desire for vengeance, and greed. At the same time, Arnold was not afraid to critique the evils of Bolshevism.

The chapter "Light and Fire," in particular, was a deliberate public statement at a decisive moment of

Germany's history. Eberhard Arnold sent Hitler a copy on November 9, 1933. A week later the Gestapo raided the community and ransacked the author's study. After the raid, Eberhard Arnold had two Bruderhof members pack the already printed signatures of *Inner Land* in watertight metal boxes and bury them at night on the hill behind the community for safekeeping. They later dug up *Inner Land* and smuggled it out of the country, publishing it in Liechtenstein after Eberhard Arnold's death. Emmy Arnold later fulfilled her husband's wish and added marginal Bible references. (Footnotes are added by the editors.)

At first glance, the focus of *Inner Land* seems to be the cultivation of the spiritual life. This would be misleading. Eberhard Arnold writes:

> These are times of distress; they do not allow us to retreat just because we are willfully blind to the overwhelming urgency of the tasks that press upon human society. We cannot look for inner detachment in an inner and outer isolation. . . . The only thing that could justify withdrawing into the inner self to escape today's confusing, hectic whirl would be that fruitfulness is enriched by it. It is a question of gaining within, through unity with the eternal powers, that strength of character which is ready to be tested in the stream of the world.

Inner Land, then, calls us not to passivity, but to action. It invites us to discover the abundance of a life lived for God. It opens our eyes to the possibilities of that "inner land of the invisible" where "our spirit can find the roots of its strength." Only there, says Eberhard Arnold, will we find the clarity of vision we need to win the daily battle that is life, and the inner anchor without which we will lose our moorings amid the mass emotions and follies of the modern age.

The Editors

Introduction

"The Living Word" fights against the dead letter.
In this final chapter of *Inner Land* my father claims
that the last persecutions of the Christians will be
undertaken with the Bible, that men with the Bible in
hand will cause heads to roll, and that the Bible is the
greatest weapon of the devil. He says that the devil
uses the Bible constantly to kill the souls of people,
and even children. He says the Bible is not the word
of God; reading aloud from the Bible is not neces-
sarily proclaiming the word of God, which cannot
be handled and printed and sold. When Jesus was
tempted in the wilderness, he said to the tempter,
"Man does not live by bread alone, but by every living
word that comes out of the mouth of God." That living   Matt. 4:4
word is the word of God, which God speaks to you
now, at this very moment, into your hearts – not what
he said to Moses or Elijah or even to Jesus. And yet the
remarkable thing is that if God really speaks to you, he
never contradicts Jesus or the prophets of God.

In reading the Bible, it is important to recognize
that it is only a witness of the word of God. The

word of God can be spoken into your heart only by
God himself. No one can speak the word of God to
someone else. God does this himself to each one and
to a whole circle. That is the wonderful experience
of the church, that the whole church hears the holy
word, hears the same gospel – not that one hears he
should go to war and fight for his country and the
other hears he should be a conscientious objector.
Formerly, the Quakers went to prison for their conscientious objection; now they believe that this is left
to each person to decide individually, and everyone is
still considered a good Christian.

In the confusion of our time, we have no possibil-
ity whatsoever of finding clarity in ourselves. All
Christians have to recognize that only God can solve
their problems – not that we are actually clear and
God will hopefully become clear. "All inner voices
that come out of the depths of our emotional hearts
are dangerous," my father writes. That is a remarkable
word!

My father tries to explain this mystery of the living
word through the writings of a servant of the word
(minister) of the early Hutterites, Ulrich Stadler, who
worked as a missionary around 1540. Ulrich Stadler
said that everything depends on faith in the Holy
Spirit and on these three articles of the Christian
faith: Firstly, God is recognized in that he is almighty
and has power over all creatures. Secondly, God is
recognized through the seriousness and justice of
the Son, Jesus Christ. And thirdly, God is recognized
through the goodness, mercy, and compassion of the
Holy Spirit.

We can understand these words only if God
speaks directly into our hearts. For instance, if we

take alone Stadler's first fact written about God the Father – that he is almighty – it is true and in keeping with the whole Bible. However, the fact that someone is almighty gives us no love to him. That Hitler with his army ran over Holland did not give Holland more love to Hitler. And yet we feel an enormous joy that God is almighty because we know he is also endlessly good and merciful and compassionate. But that cannot be learned by rote.

My father writes that if we want the word that Jesus spoke to become truth in our hearts, we must first experience pain and inner poverty and suffering. We must first be willing to carry his cross. Jesus said to Nicodemus, a man who came to him at night, that man must be born again. This new birth brings new life. When this living word is born in our hearts, it wants to live in love, and it wants to live in God alone.

John 3:1–8

God is a living God, and a living God wants to be honored by living hearts. That is why I am not for a Sunday school where the children are taught prayers by rote. I am very much for children praying in the evening and in the morning, but if you make a "must" out of it, they hate it; they do not love it. And then you have just the opposite of a prayer from the heart, which God actually wants. I am for the Bible; the Bible is good. But it has to come alive in our hearts – even the Bible itself teaches us this.

There is no higher created thing than the Bible, but it still belongs to creation and is not God himself. One could not put God in bookstores and sell him for twenty dollars apiece. But certainly when God speaks in our hearts, what he says never contradicts the words of Jesus. He will never say anything to us that is against what Jesus said or the opposite of what

Jesus said. "The Holy Spirit will remind you of every

John 14:26

word that I have said to you." And that happens: every Christian can experience this, or has experienced this, many times.

So let us honor and praise God and ask him to give us always a living church – never a dead rule, a dead letter, or a dead law, not even in the most wonderful things like community of goods. To gather treasures for oneself on earth is only a burden. Community of goods is such a wonderful solution, but even that, if it becomes a dead law, is deadening. Only God can save us from this. I wish so much for a living, fresh wind to blow so that everything cold and old and "law" is swept away by this living wind of God.

The light of the true Christ shines in all people who are open for the living word. It is not learning the Bible that makes us living. The Spirit of God explains the truth. The word begins in every believer, invisibly, and we don't need to watch ourselves to find out whether the living word is being born in us. When a baby is born, it does not watch the procedure. A new life is suddenly there.

If we have an inner need, an inner darkness, then we will only find healing by accepting the living word of Jesus. If his word is to bring healing, it must come from his heart and go into our soul and heart. Then the open book of the Bible suddenly becomes a flaming book. Every letter is like fire. Christ comes into the heart as fire and hot coals – it can be compared to the tasting of salt, it is so very real.

To proclaim the word, it is not enough to go to university and divinity school; that is not even needed. Just be a very lowly person and live from the heart.

Then it is no longer a question of our human theories and theology and the world of our own thoughts; rather, Jesus himself comes and gives us his healing medicine, and we receive him in person.

Hans Denck, Sebastian Franck, and Ulrich Stadler speak of eighty places in the Bible where two passages contradict one another in the sharpest way. Both passages must be true, for God deceives no one. If we listen to the Spirit deep down in our innermost heart, then we will understand the truth. If we listen to the intellect only and let the contradictions stand, then we are still far from the truth of God. The Bible is completely closed to the scholarly approach. Only the Master has the key to this book. He is the truth, who was with God from the beginning and who became flesh at the appointed time. He is the center of understanding and he is the life. Without Christ himself no one can understand the truth.

Inner Land had a very sad fate. My father died before he could finish it. The book was buried in the earth in metal boxes at the Rhön Bruderhof for a long time so that the Gestapo could not get hold of it. Then it was transported to the Alm Bruderhof. At the Cotswold Bruderhof and the Wheathill Bruderhof it was not translated, apart from one chapter, "The Peace of God." People did not feel the depth of this book speaking to them at that time. Still, almost every sentence could be written out in gold letters and put on the wall.

This entire last chapter of *Inner Land*, "The Living Word," throws a light on the problems of the twentieth century. Today governments are in a terrible turmoil, also in America. But we do have freedom to live in community and to refuse military service, and for that we can be infinitely thankful – also that until now we have had no Adolf Hitler. But America is in such confusion and moral decadence and there has been so much lying that one might well be afraid that an Adolf Hitler could rise to power. May God protect us from that.

I feel a very strong urge and wish for all true believers that the presence of Jesus and his living word be in their hearts. Without the presence of Jesus through the Holy Spirit, community life will become dead. Actually, the world should come to faith through our unity, and there is hope in that. This means there is a great urgency for us to give a witness. It has to become an attack on war, disunity, and murder. Love and unity have to be stronger than the spirit of this world, if only in a very small circle.

J. Heinrich Arnold

1975

The Living Word

Jesus is the life-creating word

Complete clarity is needed for carrying out the
highest vocation. Therefore every appeal for inwardness is a rousing challenge to seek this clarity. But
only God can bring about an inner awakening; only
his will is clear. Only God gives us the one pure light
that can cope with all that may arise in a dark future.
Nothing in our own nature can help us to come
to real clarity out of our deep confusion. All those
"inner voices" that speak from the bottom of our own
emotional hearts are dangerous. They are often will-
o'-the-wisps. They flicker up out of swampy ground
and lead the traveler astray.

As heirs of fallen mankind, we show our old nature
again and again. On our own, therefore, we can never
achieve anything except unclarity. There is only
one hope: the sun must rise and cast its enveloping
radiance on the swampy lowlands. Only in the light
of day does false light grow dim. Jesus brings in the
day and ends night. He is the morning star of the

dawning day and brings the old mankind to an end. Jesus is the founder of a new race – early Christianity called itself the "third race." He is the last Adam: the new man reveals himself as the new forefather. As the inner light he shines out, and as the creative word he brings into being the new man of creation's new day.
John 1:1–14 He is the enlightening and life-begetting word.

God's word is revealed in the Trinity

There is only one way to reveal the mystery of the creative word: in the unity of the Creator with Christ
1 Cor. 2:9–10 and his Spirit. In the early days of the brotherhood movement in Reformation times, Ulrich Stadler wrote his "True Christian Teaching on How to Judge Interpretations of the Holy Scriptures,"[1] in which he points to the power of the Holy Spirit and to the testimony of the three articles of the Christian faith as being vitally important for clarity; God's word, like God himself, can also be understood only in the unity that is clearly differentiated in the Father, the Son, and the Spirit.

First of all, according to Ulrich Stadler, God is recognized as God through his omnipotence – he is the Father of all creation. Next, God is recognized through the earnestness and righteousness of the Son; and thirdly, through the loving-kindness and compassion of the Holy Spirit. Rational people recognize the Creator of heaven and earth through the works of nature. They see in creation unmistakable proofs of God's omnipotence as the power of the Father. All God's works indicate that there is a God.

---

1   Ulrich Stadler, died 1540, quoted from an old Hutterian "epistle book" given to Arnold by Hutterites in Manitoba, Canada. In the following paragraphs, Arnold quotes this document directly or paraphrases.

Yet people still lack something decisive when giving honor and glory to God: the hallowing of God's name, which arises out of the second article of faith, out of the justice and righteousness that the Father fulfills in Jesus Christ and in the corporate body of all his members, the church. Thereby the third and last article is revealed: the infinite loving-kindness and compassion of the Holy Spirit! Nowhere else, and in no other way, can the word of God be recognized and grasped.

Rom. 5:5

If we are to gain knowledge of the living Son, we must expect God to do in us what was done to Christ. We must carry the cross of Christ and follow in his footsteps if his word is to become alive in us. The word must become true in deed and in reality. The works of Jesus Christ, the truth and righteousness of the crucified Son of God, are the means by which the word is revealed. In our own persons, we must submit to all three articles of faith if we are to recognize the highest good. The word as a whole must be received, living, into our hearts – it does not bestow itself in part. It must become flesh and live in pure and open hearts through the Holy Spirit. But this does not happen without great fear and trembling, as with Mary when the angel told her of God's will. The word must be born in us, too, and it can come about in no other way than through pain, poverty, and misery, within and without.

1 Pet. 2:21

Matt. 16:24

New birth brings new life. When the word is born, when it has become flesh in us, we live for love itself and for the fruits of love: we live for God alone. So our hearts are at peace. So, as the church of Jesus Christ, we become mother, brothers, and sisters of

Matt. 12:48–50 God. Then the third article of faith will be revealed: the loving-kindness and compassion of the Holy Spirit. No one can come to him save through the deep waters of need and distress. Through the bath

Titus 3:5–6 of rebirth, we are born anew. We become children of God, a brother or sister of Jesus Christ. We are awakened from the dead, led out of hell, and made alive in Christ. Through the cross we receive Christ; now we can confess that Christ has come into the flesh, for

Gal. 5:16–22 Christ lives in us. All who have experienced this are

1 John 16:13–14 ruled by the Holy Spirit. Through the word of God, the third article of faith appears in them. The Holy Spirit rejects in them everything of the world. He lives in them as the living word of eternal truth.

The true light – Christ – shines in all people who are given an understanding of the living word through suffering and the cross. Then they all see the loving-kindness and compassion of God. No one can really see or recognize God's love as long as the heart is wrapped up in worldly pleasures. But through the

1 John 16:13–14 Holy Spirit, the living word can in truth be seen, for he brings the crucified Christ into our life; in his light the whole of scripture, with all the words and sayings of God and Christ, is encompassed in the unity of the Trinity. In this unity the scripture speaks of the true, godly life; and in the Spirit we shall see how to achieve it. The living word will place it before our eyes even though it may not be written on the pages of the Bible in front of us. All those who have the Spirit of God are able to discern all things through this one Spirit.

The Holy Spirit plants the living word – Christ – into the heart of the believing church. Christ, as the inner word in all believers, is in perfect accord with every line written by his apostles and prophets, who were filled with the same inner word. For it is they who in truth give witness to him as the giver of life. John 5:39 The word comes to life in the heart of every believer. John 6:63 It is essential to grasp in our innermost being the eternal, the living Christ as the life-giving word. Christ himself, as the word coming to life, is the 2 Pet. 1:19 morning star and sun of the believing heart.

Only through the light of Christ, who is the word, can our inner lives in their darkness be freed from all their inborn unclarity. The word of God falls into the hearts of erring mortals to flood them through and through with the divine Spirit and with Christian life. From within, the living word shall transform everything. People who are becoming dead and insensitive shall themselves experience a living increase from the word as soon as their inmost hearts follow the radical call from God that has roused his people throughout all ages: "Turn your hearts to all the words I testify to Deut. 32:46 you this day."

The only way to help our failing life regain health is to prepare our hearts for the living word. A doctor's visit can help only when the patient takes the doctor's words to heart and disregards none of the instructions or medicines. Above all, the foolish patient must stop trying to cure himself with his own ideas or with neighborly advice. Our hearts can be healed only if we accept all the words of him who said: "I am the Lord, your Physician." "The medicine must be taken Exod. 15:26 internally. Outside us it does no good." The inner word brings the helpful Physician, who is himself the healing medicine. The best physician is the One who brings healing by the mere fact of his living presence. When, in an inner way, we eat and drink the life-giving word, it means that the Healer and his healing have been accepted.

1 John 4:14

This is the context in which we must see the mystery that drove so many of Jesus' friends away from him: "Unless you eat the flesh of the Son of Man, unless you drink his blood, you have no life in you!" This stark way of expressing inner union with Jesus himself was bound to turn away from him all those who were not resolved to win through to final unity with him, cost what it may. Only one who, like Peter, had experienced the power of Jesus' living word could once and for all reject the idea of leaving him: "Lord, where shall we go? Thou hast words of eternal life."

John 6:53

John 6:68–69

The Savior enters into us; we must take his words to heart, take in the Savior himself, if we are not to give ourselves up for lost. If his word is to heal, we must have it close to our heart and let it burn in our soul. The word lies before us like an open book of glowing truth on a table at which we read and work with heart and soul. Every letter shall become living fire in our hearts. Only through the heart do we receive the word like the tasting of the tongue and the searing heat of flame.

And yet ultimately, it is not through any activity of the human heart that the inner content and value of the word become alive. True, when the word penetrates our heart it awakens our innermost being, which is the first stage of inner growth. For how could we believe in the Living One if we had not heard of him? We do hear him with the awakening ear of the heart, and slowly faith arises! But the decisive hour is when we come to that faith which only God can give. Faith in God means awakening from the dead. Like Mary, faith holds on to the living seed of the Holy Spirit, the word of God at work within us. In every living word, God and God alone is at work.

The word must be born in our hearts

Through the virgin mother of Jesus, Peter Riedemann shows how the word becomes alive in the heart of a believer:

> As soon as she believed, she was sealed with the Holy Spirit. . . . The Holy Spirit worked together with her faith so that the word she believed took human nature from her. . . . Through the union of the Holy Spirit with Mary's faith, the word was conceived and became human.

Eph. 1:13

Luke 1:30–38

> The birth of Christ took place through the proclamation of the word. Mary believed the angel and received the Holy Spirit through faith. The Spirit worked together with her faith so that she conceived Christ, and he was born of her. Whoever wishes to be born in the Christian way must first, like Mary, hear the word and believe it. [2]

Whoever wants to be born of God must keep in mind how Christ's birth took place: it was brought about by the working of the Holy Spirit in faith. Every birth from God happens in the same way. When the word is heard and then believed, faith is sealed with the Holy Spirit; the Holy Spirit renews us and makes

---

2 *Peter Riedemann's Hutterite Confession of Faith* (1542) translated and edited by John J. Friesen (Plough, 2019), 68, 102.

us new creatures in the life of God's justice. We are formed in God's image. Where his word is believed, God makes it alive through the gift of the childlike Spirit. All who believe God's word will have their faith affirmed in such a living way by the imparting of the Holy Spirit that they will be renewed by it, 2 Cor. 5:17 virtually born anew. Through the living word, they will live from now on in the holy, divine life of the kingdom of God.

Faith arises from proclamation, but proclamation Rom. 10:17 comes from the word of God. The life-creating word is there first. Faith comes second, decisive for each one personally. It is an awakening from the dead when we receive the word of God into our hearts. Then the word must come to life. Faith holds firmly to the word, as Mary did. Like a seed that is germinating, it must remain in the heart and yet blossom forth in life. From its roots in the depths of the soul, the word must spread far and wide. From deep within, the word stimulates all faith's influences and furthers all the deeds of faith. The life-giving word is plainly to be seen in the growth it produces.

Without the Spirit, the law is dead

The Holy Spirit gives life to the word; through it, he produces the works of his love. He is not forced by the dead law – an alien power. He is the living finger of God himself, writing his loving word on living flesh, 2 Cor. 3:3 on the pages of the heart. The word of the Spirit is the living and working word, for it pierces soul and Heb. 4:12 spirit. It destroys the works of the devil and consummates the work of God. All who want to inherit the promised kingdom must be born through the living word. Through the Spirit, the word is planted in the innermost core of living people. All those in whom the word is active through the Holy Spirit, from the smallest to the greatest, know the living God and the kingdom where he is at work. John 3:5

What the dead law demanded in vain is spiritually alive and given its highest meaning through the word of the Spirit. In the Spirit's divine order of life, everything is accomplished in the living power of God. The written law, insofar as it is bound to the letter, is annulled through Christ, for he has given his Spirit, who has nothing dead about him. The living word leads to repentance from all dead works. The letter is dead and spreads death. If the Spirit does not accompany it, the scripture can never achieve the righteousness that counts before God. Through the Spirit of freely given and newly created life, we become free forever from the law and from all dead works belonging to the law. Once we live in the Spirit, we are no longer under the law. Rom. 8:3 Rom. 7:6 2 Cor. 3:6

We cannot have the freedom given by community in God without the word alive within us. The power of the word and the obedience born of faith free us from slavery to the letter of the law. They lead to a life where only love is at work, and love is freedom. The righteousness born of faith knows the source of its life. "The word is near you, very near; it is on your lips and in your heart." When the word becomes very dear to our heart, there is freedom and life. It has decisive significance whether we only look up the "word of God" and consider it, only hear it and read it, only understand it and think about it, only approve of it and acknowledge it, or whether we receive it and Rom. 10:8

cherish it in the innermost depths of our hearts as a living seed of God. What use is it to contemplate the source, if we do not drink from it? What use is the word if we know it only by rote and the all-too-familiar letter stays outside us? The roots of a living flower absorb the water and keep it. Out of the depths, the water must bring life to every fiber. The living word has the same effect as living water: its life wells up and flows into every branch.

Therefore Jesus said, "I give living water. Whoever drinks of the water I give him, he will never thirst in all eternity: the water I give him will become in him a spring pouring out into life, into eternal life." The living word of the Spirit is the source of life in the heart of each believer. Christ is at work in each heart as the living word that conceives, gives birth, and bears within it the powers of divine life. In the rebirth that takes place through the word of the Spirit, the life of eternity begins, never to be repressed again.

John 4:14

The seed of the word, hidden within, is stronger than anything else. It asserts its life against any shape or form of death. It overcomes any poisoning at the root. It cuts until it separates soul and spirit. The living word divides life from death. It warns against all destruction and awakens all that the divine life demands. It judges all our thoughts and feelings, shedding light on our true selves. It is radiant with the light of him who is himself life. The inner word is the inner light. It brings salvation from everything that darkens. It is the word that brings healing and salvation. It carries us to God's kingdom of light. Implanted in our innermost heart, it blossoms as the shining tree of life.

1 Pet. 1:23

Col. 1:12–13

In place of the rank growth of the life of our own ego, the garden of truth grows from within as the love of God. The world of men is the field of the living seed. In this world, the word of life makes God's will a reality. God's planting is the divine word. His seed springs from his heart of light and fights against the seeds of darkness. As the living word within grows and bears fruit, it tolerates no weed of human works. The inner word, becoming deed, fills every corner of the heart. It takes over the whole of life until everything harmful to God's planting is crowded out.

Everything that does not grow out of the seed of the new planting belongs to the soil, which still contains many other seeds of the old field with all its weeds. Only the new seed is fruitful. What happens there is a miracle: though the field remains poor and barren, the new seed grows. The living word, which goes out from God, is different from the feeble speech of humans, different from the barren letter they write. It is the living seed of God's kingdom, which like a mighty tree wants to spread over the whole world. Mark 4:30–32 The word of truth is God's living heart, the creative God himself, for it is the Christ who rules over all.

The word becomes flesh

The chaos of the old, corrupt existence is revealed through the eyes of the One who is alive and at work as the new word. As the Spirit of Jesus Christ, the Gen. 1:1–3 living word hovers over the deep and formless void. John 1:1–3 His glance reveals the creative might of God's love that completely restores all true life. The light of the new creation shines out from the eyes of Him who speaks from within the Living One. Jesus is God speaking.

Christ is the living word of God's heart. The new fire
of his word is the love of God. When the word of
Christ is received and accepted by his loving church,
there arises an indescribable joy in the Holy Spirit, in
God, and in his new creation. The church lives in this
joy and exultation that comes from the creative word
of the Spirit, giving glory to Christ in God.

The unmistakable sign that Jesus is alive in a
person's heart is the working of the creative word. It
shapes the whole of life to accord with the Spirit and
1 Cor. 2:15–16   the mind of Christ. He, who is truth at work, embraces
all truths of the divine life. The word of truth in all
its facets represents that the whole Christ must be
John 17:17   testified to. Faith is nothing less than its object: Jesus
Christ, the living content of the word. Through a mys-
terious and complete unity, receiving the living power
of the inner word becomes identical with accepting
John 1:14   the direct and living presence of Jesus Christ.

The word of God was already alive at the beginning of all things, before the first pages of the Bible
were written. The word revealed the creative and
loving nature of the one who spoke it. God's word
is God's means of revelation and his creative power.
Like the wisdom of God, it is alive and powerful. It is
God, for it is God's Spirit and God's Son – it is Christ.
It was of divine nature before the very beginning and
remains completely one with God far beyond the end
of all things. Nothing came to life without the activity of the creative word, which is more alive than all
created life. The word itself was born: it became flesh
as the one who was to reveal the free gift of divine
life. It dwelt among us. In Jesus Christ it revealed the
whole truth of God as the perfect love of his heart.

Even now, after the last page of the Bible has been

written, the word remains the living, creative word, as it was in the beginning and shall be after the end of all things. The word is alive as the Living One born of God, who enables God's innermost nature to step out of itself. The word, in all its creative working, is one with the living God and his eternal love. All living things live in him alone. As God's free gift, the word takes on shape and form. It brings the kingdom of God. It fills the church and builds it up. It dwells in the heart of God's temple and fills all the envoys of the city of God with spirit and with life.

The word reveals the truth in love – it discloses the love in truth. It speaks directly from the heart of God to the heart of the believer. It speaks in the Spirit. What it gives and what it demands has absolute authority, for the word of Christ is the truth. Its absolute "thou shalt" is no law, bound to the letter; it is alive in an ardent longing of the heart – in the holy "thou must" felt by all those in whom it has kindled its love. It is not a dry precept but a living urge. It is not a sinister threat but the radiant light of inmost liberation. It is not the letter, it is life: it is Spirit, it is Christ, it is God.

John 8:32

At the time of the Reformation, the living word burst forth once again with undreamed-of power. Next to Peter Riedemann, it was Ulrich Stadler who recognized most clearly the essential unity between the word of the Spirit and Jesus Christ. He testified:

> It is not enough to say that the word became flesh and dwelt among us. Christ must also come into our flesh. Now we must confess that Christ has become flesh in us and that our flesh is ruled by the word through the Holy Spirit. All worldly pleasure is

renounced, as Paul says: "I live, yet not I but Christ lives in me. The world is crucified to me and I to

Gal. 2:20

the world." Whoever knows Christ thus may rightly boast that he has the inner word and can truly testify to the truth. . . . All the others who come without this confession and who do not get beyond the shouting of the external sound come without Christ. He does not yet live in them.[3]

No one should preach without the Spirit

Without the Holy Spirit and his living word, without the annihilation of our old life, our own life, without the reality of a new life in Christ, no one should dare to preach the word of God. In his *Confession of Faith*, which is the confession of all the Hutterian brothers, Peter Riedemann summarizes this statement of the truth very clearly:

That is why Christ did not want his disciples to go out until they had received the Holy Spirit and had

Luke 24:46–49

been endued with strength from on high. There are some who do not wait for this gift from God but go ahead by themselves without this grace, for the sake of worldly honor or for possessions. These are the ones of whom the Lord says, "I have not sent these prophets, yet they ran; I have not spoken to them, yet

Jer. 23:21

they prophesied." For this reason their preaching is fruitless, and their teaching is not of Christ.[4]

Because they lack the Spirit, they do not have Christ's teaching. If the word is to be a message and bear

---

3 Ulrich Stadler, "The Living and Written Word," in *Anabaptism in Outline*, edited by Walter Klaassen (Plough, 2019), 146. In the following section Arnold develops ideas taken from Stadler.

4 Riedemann, *Confession*, 86.

fruit, then it must come about through the Holy
Spirit. Christ's teaching and mission must never be
mixed with the human will, but must be represented
through the Holy Spirit alone. The holy men of the
old covenant spoke as they were prompted by the
Holy Spirit. All the more now, the members of the   2 Pet. 1:21
church must speak and teach in the way the Holy
Spirit prompts them. They have to do what he brings
about through them and neither do nor say anything
of themselves. Christ puts it in these words: "It will
not be you that speak, but my Father's Spirit will   Matt. 10:20
speak through you."

In this and no other way can the word be living
and bear fruit. This truth applies to everything that
is word, to everything said or sung before people and
before God in the church of the Spirit. Like the word
that is taught and the word of mission, like prayer and
worship, so the word in songs is alive and powerful
only when the songs of the church are composed
through the Spirit of God, through his prompting.
Songs other than those of the Spirit do not belong in
the church. Those songs created by the impulse of the   Eph. 5:19
Spirit may be sung only through the movement of the
same Spirit from which they originally came.

All those who belong to the Spirit think about
what is of the Spirit. Whoever speaks, or prays, or
sings in this alert Spirit considers every word – what
it leads to and how far it goes. In such a person, the
Spirit himself is concerned and watchful to see that
everything serves to build up the one work that is
the Spirit's cause alone. The Holy Spirit makes the
word live by bringing Christ and the clarity of his
all-embracing witness into the heart and by revealing

the whole future of his kingdom – the kingdom that encompasses all worlds. The Spirit of truth reveals the teaching of Jesus as light and clarity thrown on all things. Everything God wants to say and bring to us is put in the right order within the context of the whole by the word of the Spirit. The Spirit shows to each and every one the place where they belong according to the will of God.

The word touches each person in the right place; it strikes where God wants to strike. Without God's Spirit there is no two-edged sword of the word. The living word that is Christ cuts through the heart. The sword of the Spirit knows how deep it cuts and what it is doing. Unless this sword does its work of separating, knowledge and life itself stay hopelessly confused. The Spirit of Christ alone leads to the right order in the teaching of truth and in the wisdom of life. Without clarification through the Spirit, the word of God, like the heart, remains sunk in confusion and darkness. If the whole of scripture were to be put before people's eyes at once, it would still bring neither fruit nor improvement unless it were done according to the directions of the Spirit who alone knows the truth. Only those who demonstrate the character and order of the Spirit in all their words as well as in all their works are servants of the Spirit.

Whoever wants to be a child of the Spirit and a servant of his truth must let the power and works of the Spirit be seen in all his words and above all in his life. Whoever presumes to preach the gospel in any other way is a thief. He offers stolen goods, which in his hands have become worthless. Whoever would run in haste without the power of the Spirit, before

John 10:8–11

Christ has seized hold of him, is a murderer. He Jer. 23:1–2
brings people to mortal ruin. His word, devoid of the
Spirit, is deadly. It reeks of decay, it stuns, it kills life.

Christ's truth does not belong to the letter, which
kills, but to the Spirit, who gives life. That is why Rom. 7:6
we may never let it pass our lips unless we have the
Spirit of God. But whoever receives the Spirit should
proclaim the word and make it known to those who
wait for the Spirit. It is the Spirit in the depths of the
heart, and only the Spirit, who grants again and again
the divine power of the living word. He comes to the
aid of the sound and letter of the spoken and written
testimony. These symbols of the word are spoken
and written down; then the same living, creative
power from which they sprang in the first place gives
witness to itself again as their real and living essence.

The spoken or written word is merely a sign
Peter Riedemann testifies clearly and with true spiritual discernment that the word of truth can be living,
powerful, and fruitful only through the Holy Spirit
of Jesus Christ, and that therefore only those who
bring the life-giving Spirit of the word with them may
use and witness to this holy word. In the same way,
Ulrich Stadler, with his profound insight into reality
in "Concerning the Living Word and Its Workings,"
gives a concise yet comprehensive "account and
distinction": signs of the living word are to him
signs of the living God – in the Spirit, in Jesus Christ
the crucified. Everything the Holy Spirit imparts
is brought about by God through this justice of the
cross. It is with God and his justice that his word is
concerned. The person who receives the Spirit in

faith submits and gives practical expression to God's justice, on the way of the cross.

Paul says to the Romans: "Faith comes from hearing what is preached, but hearing comes through the word of God." The right preaching and writing are not themselves God's word; rather, God's word precedes them and brings them into being. It is people filled with the Spirit of God and the power of the word (outwardly invisible and inaudible) who write and speak what the eye can read and the ear can hear. But faith and the word itself – the word that is believed – are of the invisible God. The outward eye does not see God or his word; the outward ear does not hear God himself or his voice. Before we can preach in the right way, we must be overcome by the true word of God in the very depths of our souls, where it is possible to see and hear what God puts there himself. Christ alone is the word of God. A servant of the word must have become really one with Christ through the suffering on the cross if he wants to give an account of the word, whose mystery is the cross of Christ.

The word preached by people is a token of the true word that God alone can speak. God speaks this word in Christ. The eternal word is not written by any person, either on paper or on tablets. It is not spoken or preached by any person, today or ever. The scripture written by the hand of the apostles and prophets and the word spoken by the mouth of true preachers all belong to God's well-made creation, which is meant to proclaim its Creator. This creation is not Christ, for he made it; it is not of itself the living word, which belongs to the Creator alone. There has

Rom. 10:17

1 Cor. 1:17–21

to be the sharpest distinction between scripture (also when spoken) and the inner word in the believing heart. Whoever wants to use scripture according to its true worth, whoever wants to give neither more nor less to it than belongs to it and is due to it, has to be aware of this sharp distinction.

The direct and living word is always of first importance. It is there whenever God himself speaks to the heart. It lives in the Spirit of Jesus Christ. The spoken and written word of the disciples of God (and of Jesus Christ) comes second. It presupposes the first and proceeds from the first – first of all we must be taught by God himself – just as, vice versa, through the stimulation of the outer word, the inner word is given whenever writing or preaching is accompanied by the power of the Holy Spirit. God himself teaches his word. Whoever hears the word speaks it and writes it down, and God himself teaches it afresh through the Holy Spirit.

John 6:45

Christ expressly commanded his apostles to proclaim the outer word: "Preach the gospel to all creatures." It is these apostles who have witnessed most clearly to the vast difference between the inner and the outer word. They point out that everything we hear from people, everything we see in creation or read in books, can never be the living word of God itself. We should not confuse an account and the retelling of it with the event of which it tells! To be an apostle of Jesus Christ means to be an ambassador of his kingdom, giving an account of it and spreading the news of the written commission of this embassy. Whoever believes the message of his embassy receives this same letter from Christ himself. The

Mark 16:15

2 Cor. 5:20

king reserves the right to commission and equip his ambassadors.

Like the water of baptism, like bread and wine at the Lord's Supper, the sound of the proclamation and the letter of the Bible are always only an image, a token of and a witness to what is really alive and important. The token points away from itself to what it stands for. It is not the thing itself, for whose sake it exists. The inner and eternal word – the living word of God – is witnessed to by the outer and ephemeral word, coming from people who are filled with the living word. We grasp this witness wherever and whenever, in the Holy Spirit, we perceive the cause to which it bears testimony. It is like an inn sign announcing with truth that there is wine in the cellar: the sign is not the wine itself.

It is in keeping with God's order that everywhere in his first creation, and also in his new creation, the physical precedes the spiritual. On the other hand everything physical at the beginning and at the end of God's way proceeds from the spiritual: God's Spirit is alive before he begins to work. However, in our world, in our creation, the physical witness of writing and speaking and the faith that comes from hearing precede the Spirit's work of inner justification or forgiveness of sin. It is only through the forgiving and renewing Christ that God himself can work. As the living word with God's authority, he brings this about in our hearts through the Holy Spirit.

In this justification, which is Christ himself and no other, the seed of God takes root as faith that proves itself powerfully before God and before all creation in times of storm. With the living word of Christ as

Matt. 13:21

the Holy Spirit, God himself gives assurance of his
justice to the hearts of the believers. They receive the
justification of Christ. The word is imparted in the   Rom. 5:1
very depths of their souls. Through the Holy Spirit,
it is written in the living flesh of their hearts by the
living finger of God. Thus they live in the obedience   Jer. 15:16
born of faith according to the directions given by
this living Spirit, according to the whole word of
God and Jesus Christ. The heart is gripped by Christ
and filled with his Spirit, who takes in hand what is
physical and material and gives it the shape and form
he demanded.

The living word produces new life

The living word of God that produces new life
through the power of faith is called the new commandment. True life is never old. The childlike life of
the Spirit can never be anything but new again and
again; it is the new life of love. What does it matter if   John 13:34
it has been written by Moses or David, by the proph-
ets or the apostles? Whatever part of their witness
becomes a new word in the Spirit and is really and
truly with us as a new beginning in God, that is the
living word within us. If it lives in us, if it rules over   1 John 2:7–8
us and brings us to a new birth, if our whole heart
and mind are so filled with the word's very nature
and with God's will in the way God himself wants
and longs for us to be filled, then all this is indeed the
living word within us: the word takes form as people
reborn in Christ Jesus. So, in the life-giving Spirit, the
whole word that has become alive is (and is called)
the new covenant: the New Testament.

The writings of the prophets of God and the
apostles of Jesus Christ testify that we must find the

everlasting word within ourselves if we really and truly want to seek nothing but the kingdom of God. It helps no one to know everything written in the scriptures. We must ourselves enter the number of those

Rev. 7:4 who are written in the book of life. We must suffer the work of justification (forgiveness of sin) in our own persons. Christ wants to bring it into our hearts and into our lives as the living word. If that does not happen, we remain dead in the same way as all worldly people are dead. Were we to know the whole Bible by heart, without the living work of God in us our confession (however loud and high-flown) would be nothing but delusion. It would not be the slightest use to us or to other people.

Anyone who surrenders himself to God as a living

Rom. 12:1–2 sacrifice, renouncing the whole world in Christ,
Gen. 15:6 hears the word of the Spirit in his heart. He believes
Luke 11:28 the word and receives it. But for anyone who has not been justified by the indwelling Christ, whose faith has not been confirmed by the living word within him, who cannot stand the test of Christ's sufferings or hold up under his cross – for such a one the word will be a dead sound, a dead letter, wherever he goes. The uplifted finger of the man who bore witness to

John 3:25 the word points to the way of the Crucified One.[5] Beside the living word of him who is the truth, the ever imperfect witness of the outward word is like a lifeless portrait beside the living person.

However loudly we try to persuade people that the confession we preach, the witness we hear, or the print we read in books is God's word, such teaching

---

5   The author seems to be referring to the image of John the Baptist in Matthias Grünewald's painting of the Crucifixion in his *Isenheim Altarpiece*, which is discussed briefly in Volume 2.

leaves people empty and dissatisfied. If the outward word is left on its own, no improvement follows. The living word of the Spirit must join it, otherwise everything remains as it was. Word and word belong together. The inner word is the true and essential one. It is God's eternal and almighty power; no one can change it; no interpretation can alter it; and in the believing person, it has the same nature and form as in God, for it is God. As God himself, it comes to believers and can accomplish all things. It opens up what is new. For this reason, John calls it the new commandment, which is the truth: "It is in him and in you!"

1 Cor. 2:5

1 Cor. 1:24

1 John 14:16–21

1 John 2:8

The word-become-flesh never is or teaches anything but the living Christ and his blessed cross. Therefore the church of Jesus Christ and her mission must challenge all people through the outer word to surrender to this one teacher, this inner teacher. People must never be allowed to keep to the outer word, otherwise scripture, preaching, and all the words used in them become idols. Words should never become false gods. They are all nothing but tools or images. They must, they will disappear when the word that never passes away finds its ultimate fulfillment. Until then they remain what they are: a picture of the true word in created things. However, what it represents and portrays is meant to be glorified in this picture.

The New Testament taken according to the written letter is, in this respect, no different from the Old Testament. Both remain a token or a testimony that must be preached or listened to, written or read – mere human accomplishments. It must all be

called the Old Testament and go on being called the
old commandment, the old law, and the old word
(whether it is from Moses and the prophets or from
the evangelists and the apostles) unless the living
Master of the inner word himself, coming to the
aid of the outward token, brings down the power of
the new covenant and with it pierces the heart and
conquers life. Without the Holy Spirit of the living
word, without the indwelling Christ and his new
commandment, without the love of Christ's living
heart, without the implanting of his cross and his new
life, all writing and all preaching remain dead letters
1 Cor. 13:1   and empty noise.

Only Christ himself can give us his life

The clarity of the Spirit given to this outstand-
ing Hutterian servant of the word, Ulrich Stadler,
surpassed the light given a few years earlier to Hans
Denck, the schoolmaster and scholar of Nuremberg
and Augsburg.[6] But even Hans Denck had testified
since the year 1525 that with his native ability he
could understand nothing of the scriptures unless the
day, the day itself, the everlasting light were to break
in: Christ had to rise in his heart if the word was
to become living. Whoever does not have the right
attitude to God, whoever is not penetrated through
and through by God's Spirit and filled with his love,
cannot understand the scriptures. If such people
honor the Bible, they cannot help making an idol of it.

Hans Denck says the scriptures are holy and
good. But as long as people have a wrong attitude,

---

6   Hans Denck, ca. 1495–1527, was an Anabaptist. In this section Arnold
    paraphrases Denck's ideas, based on a book from his own publishing
    house: Adolf Metus Schwindt, *Hans Denck: ein Vorkämpfer undogma-
    tischen Christentums 1495–1527* (Neuwerkverlag, 1923).

they cannot use the scriptures as they are meant to be used. The scriptures witness to Christ, but only Christ himself can give us his life. It is love that in Christ commanded what was to be written and continues to command what still could be written. In the Jesus of the Gospels, in the Christ witnessed to in the whole of scripture, the love of God is deed and reality. Through the same Christ, God's love wants to become deed and reality afresh in us! We must wait for love if we want the truth.

John 3:16

> Whoever will not wait for a revelation from God within his breast but presumes himself to undertake that work which belongs alone to the Spirit of God and Jesus Christ, will quite certainly make the mystery of God contained in the scriptures into a horror and abomination in the sight of God.[7]

Therefore, Denck continues, it is for the Holy Spirit alone to interpret the scriptures; they came from him, for he existed first. Our own interpretations and the false faith that results, the absolutely wrong and human ways of understanding the scriptures, will give way to true faith and to interpretation in the Holy Spirit only when we long for this pure faith from God himself. Therefore Hans Denck cries out to God: "Lord, I wish to have faith. Help me to come to faith!"

Mark 9:24

He recognized what is alone able to bring faith and the word of God into our hearts: only when Christ, the sun of righteousness, rises in our hearts will the darkness of unbelief be overcome. The almighty word of God can be grasped in no other way than when it comes in Christ directly from God above and pierces

Mal. 4:2

---

7 Schwindt, *Hans Denck*, 24.

Luke 1:78 the heart. By human ways and means we never come to an understanding of the holy scriptures. For it is the scriptures that testify to the wonder that is God, which no one can understand.

Like Ulrich Stadler and Sebastian Franck,[8] Hans Denck, citing eighty passages of scripture, points out how often two texts in the Bible seem to contradict each other sharply. To such an apparently insurmountable difficulty he has this to say:

> Both passages of scripture must be true, for God's Spirit deceives no one. This would be clear to us if we paid heed to the one and only teacher, the Holy Spirit, for he reveals in our innermost hearts the truth that is completely united in itself. Whoever leaves two passages contradicting each other, unable to unite their truths in God's irrefutable truth, lacks the chief thing – the ground of truth, Christ in God.[9]

Matt. 11:25 The Bible is closed to the scholarly approach. The Master alone has the key to this book, which contains all the treasures of wisdom. He is the truth; everything in this book comes from him as the only treasure that is truly good: the word, which from the beginning was with God and which later became flesh. Hans Denck impresses it on his listeners and readers with the greatest zeal:

> I testify to the future coming of Jesus Christ, our Lord, and pray that all of you who hear the truth of God, see it, or otherwise perceive it might receive it in the truth of Christ. That means you shall receive

---

8 Sebastian Franck, 1499–ca. 1543, was a Reformer and mystic. A free thinker, he did not join any of the numerous religious sects of the time.

9 Schwindt, *Hans Denck*, 52.

it in the one manner, in the one way, and in the one form that Christ taught and established! The means to all knowledge and all life is Christ, whom you cannot know in truth unless you follow him with your life.[10]

There is only one testimony to the truth. That testimony is in Christ, and it is life surging directly into us. The word living in our hearts through Christ should never be denied; we should earnestly and diligently listen to one thing: what God wants to speak in us through Christ. At the same time, of course, we should not absolutely reject all outer witness; we should rather hear and test all things; we should compare them in the reverence born of the Spirit. If we do that, our understanding of the truth will grow purer from day to day until at last we hear God himself without human words; we hear no one but God speaking to us, God alone, "God absolutely unconcealed."[11] Only then shall we be certain what his will and nature is.

We cannot reach heaven in our own strength
Only those who have the living law of truth written in their hearts through the Holy Spirit have received the new covenant, the living covenant of God. Only such people are truly just, for righteousness belongs to God alone, to the living Spirit that is not human and doesn't come to us through people. All righteousness of our own collapses. If someone is presumptuous enough to think he can walk straight up to heaven in his own strength, he will fall and plunge in the

Eph. 2:8–10
Rom. 9:16

---

10 Schwindt, *Hans Denck*, 38.

11 Schwindt, *Hans Denck*, 35.

opposite direction. "But if I walk in the strength of truth, so that not I walk but the word of God in me and therefore – impelled by the word – I walk in the way of suffering, then my walking will not be in vain."[12] God himself sees to it that his righteousness takes its course in the free will of believers in him. God alone can make us want his word and the works of his right-

Phil. 2:13 eousness, and he alone can bring their fulfillment.

To believe means to be obedient to the word of God, come life, come death. Whoever believes follows God with the utmost confidence that everything his

Rom. 8:28 Spirit prompts in us will lead to the best. Those who have been sent out on their journey by God know God; their word is one with God's word. They realize that there is no contradiction in God. They are able to grasp that the living word in believing hearts is in complete agreement with all the prophets and with all the apostolic scriptures. This is the goal we must reach – the unity of the truth.

We must rest from all our own works in God himself so that he and his living word alone can work and rule in us; God himself will teach us his ways most wonderfully. In short, all Christians (that is, those who have received the Holy Spirit) are one with Christ in God; they are so united among themselves in the unity of his word that what concerns one concerns all. Therefore, what Christ did they also do,

John 17 and in their unity they have Christ as their one Lord and Master.

The truth has always stood revealed in God's heart. He showed the truth to his prophets at all times, but through Jesus Christ it was revealed again

---

12 Schwindt, *Hans Denck*, 34.

to all people, this time in all its fullness. He became man and took a sacrificial death on himself for this reason, that from now on through his Spirit all people everywhere would have the one united witness of the truth. God has been good from the very beginning. In Christ, he lets his loving-kindness be known to all people – he never conceals it. Wherever trust in the loving-kindness of God's heart arises through the living word of God, wherever trust grows out of our earth – from us worldly people – truth as love and justice looks down from heaven on us all. Christ reveals the heart of God!

2 Cor. 5:19

Ps. 25:6

As soon as the justice and righteousness of God have come to us in Christ as the living word, we realize that it is not we but rather the Spirit of God, dwelling in us and at work in us, who has given back to the Father what we had stolen from him. From that moment on there is peace – as unity with God, unity with his apostles and prophets, and unity among ourselves. Yet free as we now are from everything else in the confidence this love gives us, precisely from this moment on we can do nothing good except "in the way of suffering": we willingly let happen to us what God does; held captive by God himself, we are able to submit in absolute freedom of will and heart to what Christ as the word does in our hearts and in our lives.

God's loving-kindness, the truth of his love and justice, the unity of his peace, and the freedom of his life (as the whole gospel of Jesus Christ) are the foundation of all that the holy scriptures testify. The writings of the Old and New Testaments are of divine origin. Therefore no one can understand them except people who are enlightened by the divine Spirit,

because only in such people does this same living
source well up. Only when our will is moved by God

John 10:27
are we in living harmony with Christ's voice, for as
John 7:17
the word of God it lives in our hearts. Then we can
understand the scriptures.

God must open the scriptures to us

Divine enlightenment takes place in the depths of
2 Cor. 4:6
the heart, and yet it is recognizable. Every evil and
unenlightened heart betrays itself through arrogance
and impatience. Every heart filled with God's loving-
kindness shows Christ's humility and the patience
of his love. If the divine Spirit is not at work in us,
cooperating with our faith, if he does not help us recognize loving humility and make it a genuine reality
in ourselves, the holy scripture – because it remains
something apart – proves a shaky foundation for faith.
Only those who bear within themselves the living
word, the divine source of all the holy scriptures, are
in living contact with the great stream of all that God
reveals: they live in the truth.

God's new covenant (clearly testified to in the holy
scriptures as a revelation of God) can be received only
by those who have the law of freedom (again, testified
by scripture) inscribed in their hearts by the Holy
Rom. 8:1–2
Spirit. But those who imagine that they will succeed
in following the law of righteousness from the Bible
itself ascribe to the dead letter what belongs to the
living Spirit. Those who want to glorify the scriptures, yet have let divine love grow cold within them,
should take heed that they do not make an idol of the
scriptures; that is what all the scribes and scholars do

who are not taught by the Holy Spirit and not led to   1 Cor. 2:13–14
the kingdom of God.

Hans Denck, therefore, has this to say:

> I esteem the scriptures above all human treasures;
> yet I do not esteem them as highly as the word of
> God, which is living, strong, and eternal, free from
> all elements of our world, whereas the scriptures are
> not. What is of God himself is Spirit and no letter. It
> is written without pen and paper in such a way that
> it can never be blotted out. Therefore salvation does
> not depend on the scriptures, however good and ben-
> eficial to that end they may be again and again. This
> is the reason: it is not possible for scripture alone to
> make an evil heart good, however well-versed in the
> scriptures a person may be. A heart is truly believing
> only where a spark of divine zeal is alive. Only a heart
> that burns in God is improved by all things. [13]

Improved, above all, by the holy scriptures. Yet Christ
alone, as the inner light, changes life. All this does not
mean that for the sake of the living word we should
neither listen to sermons nor read the scriptures,
for the scriptures testify to the truth. But, Denck
continues, what is most important for each person, as
scripture sees it, remains the following:

> Not what I am and do, but what truth itself reveals,
> as I sense it within me – this I know for certain is the
> truth. Therefore I will listen to truth speaking, God
> willing, and hear what it says to me; and I will let no
> one take it from me.

---

13 Schwindt, *Hans Denck*, 58. Compare Denck in *Anabaptism in Outline*, 142.

So there is nothing said here against the scriptures but against human arrogance toward the scriptures:

> To the extent that I dare approach the scriptures out of my own ability, I understand nothing. To the extent that I am driven by truth itself and its life-giving Spirit, to that extent do I comprehend the holy scriptures; but then not out of my own ability and merit but out of God's grace.

First of all, the foundation of faith must be laid; then everything built on it can resist wind and water.

Matt. 7:24–29

> In God's sight the foundation has long been laid, but you have to know where this foundation should be laid for *you*: namely in the temple and throne of the divine glory of Jesus Christ that should be your heart! The justice and righteousness of God remains God himself; everything that rises up against God in your heart or in your life must be sin to you.

1 Cor. 3:10–16

Your life will show whether God's word is living in you. Good works are never achieved without God being at work in the heart; you cannot do them of yourself. God will do them in you through Christ.

Yet God forces no one. Long ago he did everything possible to help us. He gave up his Son, Jesus Christ to a sacrificial death. God made Christ the means to all liberation and union. We can accept him or we can reject him – he remains the same. He wants nothing but the love, freedom, and unity that he himself is. Christ paved the way that no one could find; now we can tread it of our own free will to reach the goal of life. The way is love. When selfishness is overcome, our hearts are won over by the gospel; we listen to it,

John 14:6

1 Cor. 13

and faith is born. Christ did not only proclaim the divine gospel to his disciples or use letters to write it down: from the beginning to the end of the world, he speaks and writes it in their hearts. Those who truly have it in their hearts are completely free and act in freedom.

In Jesus love is perfected [14]

All who are truly disciples of Christ have a living word in their hearts – the fiery, loving word whose liberating strength loves nothing but God alone. This word leads them; all they do and all they leave undone is directed according to this burning love. Even if they had nothing in writing, they would have to do what this love commands. All written laws must give way to love; they were given for love's sake, not love for theirs. Laws are made and broken. But true love is the one God, who cannot create himself although he created all things, who cannot break himself although he will break all things. He is uncreated, unbreakable love. In this or that person – in the one more, in the other less – a living spark of this love can be felt, for God, as love, did not want to stay far off. Unfortunately, in our times this fiery spark seems extinguished in almost everyone. Yet Christ is still the radiant word of love!

Quite certainly, the smallest spark of love in us, however dimly it may glimmer, never comes from us but exclusively from the perfect love that is God himself: love is spiritual, whereas all people are

Eph. 3:17

1 John 3:18

---

14 This section is based on Denck's words in *Von der wahren Liebe* (Menno-nitische Verlagshandlung, 1888), available in English in *Early Anabaptist Spirituality*, translated and edited by Daniel Liechty (Paulist Press, 1994), 112–121.

carnal. Often the spark is very dim, and only perfect love can help. Now the one man in whom love has been proved to be perfect and at its most sublime, Jesus of Nazareth, is the savior, redeemer, and healer of his people in accordance with the will of eternal love. Through the power of the Holy Spirit, he showed publicly by all he did or left undone what befits love. He has been proved to be the promised savior in the midst of Israel. He it is who was promised by the true God in the holy scriptures and was brought forth when his time was come, in accordance with the promise. In Christ Jesus, perfect love conquers the human race.

1 Pet. 2:22–24

In these loveless times, we recognize that what is now scarcely to be felt really came to fulfillment long ago in Christ Jesus. Through the Spirit of God we know for certain that God's love toward us, and our love toward God, can never be more sublimely shown than it was in Jesus. In the living word of the Spirit, we are certain that God in his compassion for the world will cast aside all the judgment his righteousness calls for in the face of our sin if only we do not despise the one thing: what took place in Jesus! In him the essence of perfect love has been thoroughly taught and sufficiently proved in the course of the history of humankind – not by people but by God.

Rom. 5:8–21

All those who have sought and found the way of God have become one with God, but this One, who never stumbled in going the way of God, was never disunited with him; from the very beginning he was at one with God and remained at one with him. Nothing else than what this one love taught and did in Christ Jesus is truly right and good. In the old and in the new law, one and the same love is hidden, but only in the new covenant is it shown at its most sublime through Jesus. Whoever longs to recognize and find true love must experience it through this Jesus Christ in the most intimate way and in no other. Love consists in knowing and loving God. That, however, takes place in Christ. His new law of life makes us children of God, which no human can do. The merciful God himself, as our one true Father, must draw us into Christ so that we are born in him in the very depths of our souls. He himself allows his children to know his innermost will through the living word of his Spirit. This is nothing less than love itself, as it came in Jesus Christ and as it shall continue to be proclaimed by the gospel of his glorious grace. The living word of perfect love is nothing less than Jesus Christ himself.

Eph. 1:17–23

Those who teach anything different from what love, and love alone, has given them do not build on the foundation of Jesus Christ. They will not be able to answer before Love for their actions. Moreover, if they happen to have recognized this foundation and source of all that is good and yet teach otherwise, they will still less be able to defend themselves before Love, which is God himself. Children of love neither say nor do, for love's sake, anything that is contrary to love. Everything that means life streams to them from perfect Love, which is Jesus Christ himself. By this it is possible to find out who has the Spirit of truth; whoever understands this and yet teaches otherwise is an antichrist; whoever does not understand it has not yet recognized Christ, the Lord. Faith is no faith where Christ is not present. Christ is God's love and his living word.

1 John 2:21–23

The new creation is not the old creation

Everything reported above about Hans Denck testifies to this one faith alone: that the loving Christ as the living word of God longs to enter our human hearts in order to bear witness there to the truth, as an impulse and revelation of the Holy Spirit, in such a way that under his direction the life and confession of all believers (each united within himself and united with the others) shall be in complete accord with the Bible of the apostles and the prophets. The revelation of the living word is the revelation of Jesus Christ, the crucified, who broke down all walls and barriers. He is unity; we cannot have it without him. Thus the faith and life stemming from his word are not inborn in any person. Faith is a completely new gift from the indwelling Christ and his Holy Spirit: God speaks the living word – Christ! "Who will give me faith? If faith were mine by nature, I would by nature have life; but I do not have it."[15]

Eph. 2:14

Sometimes what Hans Denck says is almost word for word in agreement with the apostolic witness of Peter Riedemann and Ulrich Stadler. In essentials they seem at first sight to be in complete agreement. Yet Hans Denck, like Sebastian Franck, leaves questions that were answered in Hutterianism: Can the witness to truth in the gathered church of Jesus Christ and the preaching of those on mission, can the written word of the apostles and prophets and all the teachings based on this written word ever become superfluous? Is the word of Jesus Christ everywhere and always clearly distinguishable from the voice of conscience inborn in the old, first creation? Is the new

---

15 Schwindt, *Hans Denck*, 23.

creation so clear and definite that it predetermines the form and shape of the material word and life, which may never be neglected – not even for the sake of the inner life?[16]

There is some unclarity when Hans Denck says that the invisible light and word of God shining in the heart of each person has been there from the beginning and has given each one the freedom and power to inherit the Father's kingdom. It even brings confusion when he says that the same word speaks clearly in everyone and in everything in heaven or on earth, not only in the blind, deaf, and dumb but also in irrational animals, in trees and grass, in stones and wood; and that all those things can "hear" the word and "do" his will. True, the creative word as the Logos in Jesus Christ is at one with the redemptive word of the Gospels. But what is blurred and dimmed in Hans Denck is the true discernment that distinguishes very sharply between the new revelation in Jesus Christ and his Holy Spirit and the work of the deeply corrupted old or first creation.

The dead letter kills

Hans Denck comes close to Sebastian Franck in this effacing of the boundaries between the old nature and the new revelation.[17] At the beginning of his spiritual development, this remarkable historian, Sebastian Franck, had met Hans Denck and his friends,[18] and

---

16 Schwindt, *Hans Denck*, 36.

17 This section is based on Sebastian Franck's ideas in *Paradoxa*, edited by Heinrich Ziegler (Eugen Diederichs, 1909), available in English as *280 Paradoxes or Wondrous Sayings*, translated and edited by E. J. Furcha (The Edwin Mellen Press, 1986).

18 In fact, Sebastian Franck married the sister of two brothers who were close friends of Denck.

he was not uninfluenced by them in the direction he took. The brothers known as Hutterian were familiar with his works, several of which they copied and faithfully preserved, as they did some of Hans Denck's. In their books they draw extensively on Sebastian Franck's testimonies to the truth. They do not mention his name, however, because their life of faith, which had been so thoroughly purified, did not tolerate being mixed with deviant ideas. They refused to be diverted in the slightest from the clarity of the word of God given to them.

Yet to try for objectivity's sake to single out the simplest and most significant truths from the rich store of ideas in Sebastian Franck's writings is daring. Sebastian Franck is hard to understand. He is no opponent of the biblical word; but he is aware that this book of God's testimony remains sealed with seven seals to the whole world unless Christ's light of life and the Holy Spirit's definitive interpretation dawn on the reader of the Bible. For Sebastian Franck the whole Bible is a cloak of letters like the parables of Jesus, which Jesus used to hide his secret so that the holy truth would not be trodden upon by unworthy feet. For Franck, the holy scriptures are nothing but fantastic and puzzling stories until the Spirit himself, who gave rise to them, expounds the letters. Until that happens, Franck sees that it must seem incomprehensible gibberish to all – a dark lantern, whose light has not yet been lit for them.

John 5:39–40

The light of the Bible is able to shine out only when our hearts are also kindled, and God alone can kindle the light. Whoever is unready to do God's will, whoever will not accept Christ's attitude, whoever does not receive his Spirit, will never be enlightened and instructed by God to understand the scriptures. Bible in hand, such a person holds nothing but a manger without the Christ Child, a wooden cross without the Crucified One, nothing more than an empty scabbard, a platter without the bread![19] All our own efforts to grasp the dead letter are in vain. There is no other key to the Bible except the key to the kingdom of God. This key is Christ and his Holy Spirit. Whoever does not have him stands before firmly locked gates. He is kept out of God's garden by the iron bars of the letter, blocking his way.

The letter makes people dull, rigid, obstinate, cold, and cruel. A man whose head is stuffed full of the leaden letters of the Bible, devoid of the Spirit, is as capable of killing the Son of God and his people as the scribes and Pharisees were; he wants to stab them with the sharpened, dagger-like letter of the scriptures.[20] To this day, all apostles and truly living members of the church of Christ are punished as liars and put to death with the help of the letter of the Bible. As long as the Bible is understood only literally, it continues to be the murderous sword of the Antichrist and the deathly throne on which he sits. The Antichrist uses the cunning dagger and the blunt, leaden sheath of the letter against the drawn sword of the Spirit. He uses the darkened lantern against the light that belongs in it.[21]

The Antichrist has the letter on his side against the Spirit of the scriptures. The black of printer's ink

---

19 Franck, *Paradoxa*, 4.

20 A reference to the Fraktur (blackletter) typeface of early Bibles.

21 Franck, *Paradoxa*, 5–6.

is his favorite color. With it, he plays off one wooden letter against another. He splits the Bible with it: he is bent on making the witness of the Bible divided within itself by means of the literal word of scripture. He tries everywhere to annihilate the most important attributes of the word: judgment, mercy, and faith-

Matt. 23:23 fulness. Those who try to represent biblical truth by excelling in knowledge of the text will become loveless by nature and godless in knowledge. Becoming more and more learned, they never become better. They fight against those who worship God. They pay court to the letter, which God appointed to serve as a tool. They render adoring service to externals that God meant to give us for our help. They have made what was meant as a picture, as a semblance or a sign, into an object of idolatry. They have set up as their god what is spoken and written according to manmade rules of phonics![22]

Those who will not ask God humbly and reverently for the true Spirit of the Bible, who will not beg for the light of the Holy Spirit to show them clearly the deepest meaning of the scriptures, will keep on being misguided and led astray by the external word. To such people the same happens as to the scribes in the time of Jesus: with all their knowledge of the Bible they did not understand the scriptures – they

Matt. 13:13 grasped neither their power nor their meaning. They understood to perfection all the words of the Bible from cover to cover, yet always from outside only! They knew everything that could be found in the holy scriptures according to the letter of human words. But not one in a thousand could grasp the

---

22 Franck, *Paradoxa*, 7.

mystery of the word hidden behind the words, which is God's mystery.

The contrast is conclusive. Service to the letter sits on the throne of Moses. It can indeed read aloud and recite biblical passages, guard and administer the Bible in a truly Old Testament fashion.[23] But it knows nothing about the new covenant of the life-giving word. Everything it repeats is stolen. Nothing it says comes from the source; nothing comes as God's free gift. Its ungenuineness denies the power of Jesus Christ and his apostles. Its works are empty and unprofitable, and all its efforts are superfluous. It hauls water to the river; it brings more and more letters where there was already more than enough preaching and writing.[24] Yet it can never bring fresh water – the life-giving word – into anyone's heart, no matter how intensely people thirst for God's flowing spring; if everything depended on service to the letter, we would die of thirst in a wilderness of dead words.

2 Tim. 3:5–8

Ps. 42:1–2

The Holy Spirit makes everything clear

God's true word works quite differently. It lives in the Holy Spirit, who is the eternal well of life. The Spirit, and the Spirit alone, gives new life to what was once written under his guidance; he makes it rise from the dead. He is the only teacher of the covenant of resurrection. Out of the confused maze of dead pages, he shows the way to the organic tree of life. He shows the way out of the fossilized grammar of human linguistics, into the living clarity of the eternally creative word. In the Spirit, Christ brings to our hearts the

John 4:13–15

---

23 Franck, *Paradoxa*, 207

24 Franck, *Paradoxa*, 212.

unanimous agreement of all God's witnesses as the spiritual unity of all living truth.

As soon as the Holy Spirit reveals the illuminating light of God's sun, the significance of God's cause, which had been obscured, becomes bright and clear. Pure white light is its color – it brings the radiant, white-hot concentration of all the bright colors of the truth. The Spirit reveals the complete accord of God's word, which is the meaning of Jesus Christ's unity. He frees us from the letter's deadly law, from division, and makes all truth living and united, united with the living Christ, united with all his prophets and apostles, united with the living church. The understanding of the scriptures given by the Spirit leads to the bond of Christ's peace: absolute unity in all living truth. The unifying light becomes visible as soon as it streams in – when light appears, it can be seen.

Ps. 36:9

Only God has command over light. The ability to give life, which is the ability of the Spirit who enlightens and unites, is unattainable by human effort – it lies within the Creator's power, and his alone! Only directly from God himself can we receive what God alone can accomplish. Whenever the personal word of Christ, the voice of the Lamb of Bethlehem, the call of the Lion of Judah, begins to speak in people, it is God who wants to consummate his work in us. In Jesus Christ, God himself descended to lost humankind. Through the Holy Spirit, the word of God became flesh of Jewish blood in Bethlehem, but not to remain flesh. It became once again creative Spirit! And yet in the Spirit the word is heard and recognized so that once again it becomes flesh: a new people drawn from all nations – the new body of Christ!

1 Cor. 12:27

In Jesus, the infinite took physical form

Jesus was the immortal word taking on mortality;
he was and is the human incarnation of the spiritual
word. He represents what is eternal and gives it
form. He is the one we must listen to, the one we   Mark 9:7
should grasp. God's eternal and everlasting word
was brought to the earth through the one Jesus who
took on human shape in time and space. What in
him became flesh and voice was the word of God
itself – the eternal rock on which the church, as
the renewed incarnation of the spiritual word, is
built – the almighty word, which is of divine nature   Col. 1:15
and created everything.

In the Spirit of Jesus Christ, God's word shows
itself afresh as God's arm and God's finger – God's
word lives, for something new is created time and
again and is there, so to speak, in a twinkling. The
unity of the first or old creation with the new creation
is given in Christ and his Spirit. Only the one word   Eph. 2
of God so establishes and restores all things that they
are kept on the path of his creative will. Were God not
to speak the word of creation or of the new creation
anymore, everything would fall back into nothing-
ness. The word that God speaks in the first creation
and in the new creation is of all things *the* thing; of all
existence, *the* existence.

Only in God's immediate presence does his word
stay unveiled. For those who have forsaken God, it
has long been sunk in concealment. Only to a few in
each epoch has the word broken through, pierced the
heart, and become audible. But when the time was
fulfilled, it was brought once again out of its deep
concealment to the light of day through Christ Jesus.
As the word become flesh, Jesus disclosed in the new

creation the vanished word of the first creation. The seals that fastened it were broken, and at long last God's letter, opened in a surprisingly new way, could be read again, bringing an overwhelming revelation with its rediscovery. The divine light no longer glimmered in the distance, enveloped in a fog that spread for miles. In Christ Jesus and the Spirit, the word as ultimate clarity emerged out of the depths of the worldwide fog into close proximity.[25]

In Christ Jesus, service in the new covenant began, near to God. The new covenant was the new revelation. The apostles of the revealed truth of Jesus Christ were sent out. To the far-off, they brought

Eph. 2:13   his nearness. Openly and clearly they testified to God's revealed mystery. Where people formerly held writing in their hands (though they decidedly did not have what they thought they had), now the ultimate was unveiled and offered to them. People were from now on doubly convinced: first of all through the testimony of the witnesses sent out, but far above everything else through the direct witness of the all-revealing Spirit in the depths of their own hearts.

With the coming of the Holy Spirit, the new covenant begins. The new word comes down to earth. Its rulership is established in the human heart, in the deepest depths of the human spirit. Whoever is in Christ, whoever is a child of truth, hears this voice within his or her innermost heart – and obeys it. So all that had formerly been quite unknown is now spoken audibly in the heart. The night is over. Where Christ – the spoken will of God – is seen and heard, day breaks in.

---

25 Franck, *Paradoxa*, 107–108.

The story of Jesus' life holds power

Now it is a question of understanding Jesus Christ
and his whole life in the written history of the
Gospels, of grasping Jesus in the records of his spoken
word! That means receiving his Spirit into the depths
of our hearts! It is a question of living according to
this Spirit in the strength of Jesus Christ! Christ   Gal. 5:16
wants to open up undreamed-of things in the hearts
and lives of the believers. What no one can believe
comes to us. With forgiveness and with the suffering
of Christ, what was unknown to all people comes to
our hearts as faith and Spirit, as the eternal nature of
God. What was always present in God's heart – the
kingdom of heaven – is opened up and given to us.   Eph. 1:7

God's Christ, who was always present but had
never yet ruled among men, is from now on given to
men. Everything changeable and transient, everything human and manmade, must give way before
him. It must vanish before the eternal and immutable
peace of Jesus Christ, in which God has opened
his heart. God's love was sent to benumbed and
frightened hearts. The almighty word came to unite
with weak people. God's love became our brother.
Jesus brought the true picture of God into our midst
and still recognized us as brothers. Everything God's
inmost heart ever was or willed among humankind
from the beginning comes to them with Christ, and   Heb. 10:5–10, 20
will in Christ be accomplished and perfected.

When this greatest event of all history took place,
it had to be written down. These holy accounts
should lead us ignorant people to believe that this
word of love that came to the land of Israel – this
Christ of Jewish history – can be grasped by men and

women of today for their present lives, that through
his holy, life-giving Spirit the same Jesus Christ is
given the same form and life again everywhere!

Here the one way becomes visible, the one door
is opened. Through Jesus – the Jesus of Roman and
Jewish history, who became flesh, was slain, and
rose again from the dead – all people can have direct
access to God. In him, all God's mysteries lie open
for all to see. Everything God does and everything
people are meant to do with God for others is given in
Christ. He who has gained mastery over human life,
through the Spirit and the word, overcomes death. He
brings the Spirit's rule, victorious over all flesh.

This is the Christ who penetrates human hearts,
coming as the peace of God's kingdom in the power
of the resurrection and with the renewal given by the
Holy Spirit. From there, he wants to lead all created
things into a life of the new justice and righteousness
of God's creation, which is Christ. Through the Holy
Spirit, his origin, his life, and his suffering – victorious over all evil – are shown again as God's
righteousness. The church is the new Christ. The
age-old Christ is risen and is present in the church
as life-giving Spirit. In the new Christ of the church,
the birth, the life, the suffering and death, and the
resurrection of the historical Christ are repeated as
the all-embracing justice of God's kingdom.

The beginning of Christ's way, its course, and
its end cannot be altered for any member of the
church. Into each member flows the unchangeable
Christ as he always was, as he is now, and as he will
be eternally! He fills all members with his death and
with his life. If we refuse to let Jesus Christ live and

Acts 14:27

2 Tim. 1:10

Matt. 22:37–39

Heb. 13:8

Rom. 6:3–11

die in us, then for us Jesus was crucified in vain. Even chopping Jesus into a thousand pieces would not help us. Nothing can help, nothing can be called the saving word of God but this penetrating of the crucified Christ into our hearts. Going out from the heart, Christ's Spirit and life determine everything as they did in the life of Jesus.

Christ alone is the purpose and meaning of the holy scriptures. Christ filled the disciples when they wrote the scriptures. He alone is the golden scale for testing the spirits. He proves that all other spirits are misleading. Only Christ's service in the Spirit writes the will of God in our hearts. As the living word, the Son reveals the Father through the Holy Spirit. In this way Christ confirms both Testaments. He alone gives them meaning by entering people's hearts with his word and life, through the new reality of his death and resurrection in the power of his Holy Spirit.

1 John 4:1–3

Matt. 11:27

John 5:39–40

Thus the history of Christ becomes a power in the present: here and now, Christ enters in, faith receives him, and we live according to his Spirit; here and now we experience in Christ that God is uniting the world with himself in the most complete way. Thus God enfolds us in his love. Thus the power of his heart is made clear. By grasping the Father in Christ, we reach the Father's heart in the Holy Spirit. In Christ, what God's heart is and what God's heart can do are made clear. In the living Spirit of Jesus Christ, God establishes his word in our hearts.

John 6:44–45

The written scripture speaks to our hearts in a way we can understand. It is directed entirely to our hearts. All it says leads to the revelation in which the Holy Spirit will be poured out over all flesh! This revelation is needed. Whatever God does and says is for its sake. The word had to be written and has to be proclaimed afresh all the time for the sake of this revelation. Christ is the revelation of God. Its perfect and most living, its first and last picture is and will be to all eternity the life of Jesus. In Jesus, God in all his fullness dwelt in a body. Jesus is the Christ. He is what he teaches. He gives what he promises. He is the source of what he reveals.

Col. 2:9

In Christ there are no masters

This revelation of God in Christ Jesus is the inner light of the Holy Spirit. From within, it illuminates the whole of life right to its outermost aspects. In the power of this light, the same deeds done by the historical Jesus will be done again. There is nothing here but Christ. The revelation of Christ as the perfect light tolerates no human light and no human work. God carries it out himself; his truth needs no human support.

This truth lets itself be neither mastered nor hindered. No one can force another person into it, nor is it within any person's power to remove it or keep it back. The truth of Jesus Christ needs no masters – what it needs is pupils. The revelation of God's truth needs simply and solely a gathering of listeners, who, without this light, sit in the dark,[26] shake with hunger, and are parched with an agonizing thirst.

Matt. 5:6

Ps. 63:1

Truly man can never be a master of the divine. He has lost the source of light that was originally given to him. Through dark covetousness, through self-will and ownership, the will to the light that used

---

26 Franck, *Paradoxa*, 347.

to flow freely in all people dried up. Of their own Jer. 2:13
free will, people deviated from the light of God's will
constantly breaking in. Alienated like this, man could
not reconcile himself to his position. He became
overbearing and presumptuous. Out of his own dark
power he wanted to steal for himself what belongs to
God alone.

But the new man, Christ Jesus, has taken upon
himself the guilt of this defection. In Christ it is
eliminated. People are reinstated into the supreme
freedom of God's will through the degradation and
suffering of the Son of God. It is for Christ's humble
love that they are won. In Christ they are freed from
covetous self-will and arrogant ownership. Having
turned away from their own darkness, they are led
toward the eternal light of the complete revelation. Isa. 53

Arrogance dies away. Dark self-will and grim
ownership are buried with Christ. From now
on everything belongs to God. In unity with
Christ – that is, with God's heart and Spirit – the
new life breaks in, the liberating light of the risen
Christ! In this revelation, all believers are brought to
complete unity; there are no masters, only brothers. Matt. 23:8
Wherever the truth is taught, God's unity exists.
Then it is God alone whom we listen to and obey, John 17:6–10
whom we allow to speak and work. Then the brothers are united, for God never contradicts himself.
The revelation of God's truth leads to the complete
unanimity that is within God himself.

Preachers must live what they proclaim

When supposedly brilliant preachers obviously
contradict themselves or each other, they prove that

they have risen before they were awakened, that they have set out before the sun came up. Without being appointed, they have taken liberties with what they do

Jer. 23:21

not understand. They have gone to work at nighttime: they want to thresh without light and have no idea what they are hitting – they thresh nothing but empty straw. They even hit out at each other; since no light has united them, they cannot work together. [27]

The Holy Spirit never brings about his life (which is creative and unites) by means of an unenlightened or disunited spirit. He uses means that correspond to the end; he does what is good only through good. He awakens life only through the alive: he proclaims the kingdom of God only through those who live it. Only those authorized by him serve the gospel. Only those servants who are filled by Christ and, as God's mouth-pieces, speak out of the Holy Spirit are able to sow Christ in people's hearts, implant and inscribe Christ

2 Cor. 3:2–3

in their innermost being, and bring Christ in renewal and rebirth. To proclaim the word of God means bringing Christ with it and imparting the Holy Spirit.

Those who bear this service, therefore, must carry everything they say as coming from the Holy Spirit within their hearts. What they proclaim, they prove in their lives by the visible working of the Spirit. As apostles of Jesus Christ, they must be able to say to others, "You are my handiwork in Christ; it was Christ who called you and recreated you when the word came to you. You are God's handiwork, just as

Eph. 2:10

I am." Actual life proves the truth of Christ's saying: "If you do not want to believe words, you must believe

John 10:38

works." Whoever believes Christ will do the same

John 14:11–12

works as Jesus and greater works than he. Love is

---

27 Franck, *Paradoxa*, 207.

mightier than anything else. Where the unity of
Christ's love is not demonstrated in harmony of word
and life, there is neither faith nor vocation to the
service of his word. Peter was not allowed to approach
the flock until he had been asked three times whether
he loved; he was not allowed to work until he had   John 21:15–19
received the Spirit of perfect love.

We need to wait for the Holy Spirit. It means
waiting for love. And it is not only at the beginning
of the way that we wait for it: whoever has once been
gripped by the Spirit of love must become the hand
and mouthpiece of God daily; he must learn again
and again to say and do everything not in his own
strength but in God's. Only in the Christ-Spirit of   2 Cor. 5:14–15
love are we given the reverence not to say or do any-
thing earlier or later than God's hour dictates – not
even to want to do it. God's word leads to God's
Sabbath, wherein we rest from all our own words and   Heb. 4:9–11
works and let God alone speak and work!

The image of God comes to light again
This glimpse into the most secret Christian recesses
of Sebastian Franck's heart proves again how closely
interwoven were the spiritual movements of Reformation times. Kaspar Schwenckfeld[28] (who twice lived in
the same city as Sebastian Franck when Franck was
at the height of his activity) even believed that Franck
had taken his (Schwenckfeld's) ideas and altered them
into poisonous errors.

But far more important is the complete agreement
between Sebastian Franck and Hans Denck in very
decisive articles of faith. The most important of the

---

28 Kaspar Schwenckfeld von Ossig, 1489–1561, defended the Anabaptists
and shared many of the ideas of the writers quoted above by Arnold.

testimonies from Hans Denck (already covered in this book) are found five or ten years later in Sebastian Franck, so we will not repeat them at this point. Whoever has followed the encounters of these two men, inner and outer, knows that Sebastian Franck, from the time when he was first moved, followed in the footsteps of Hans Denck.

This is also evident in the most difficult and important question both men had to face as part of their actual task in life: "What relationship in the believer's heart does the hidden breath of the first word of creation have to the new revelation of Christ?" According to Sebastian Franck, a faint trace of the breath of God lives in every human, Christian or heathen. He maintains that God's word and nature is in all his creatures even though God himself stands above them in sovereign freedom and even though as the pure, good, and loving one he can never have been the origin of the evil inherent in them.

According to Franck, it is through the serpent, who is God's enemy, that man's free will was corrupted and turned into self-will. Through the serpent's poison, man was weakened and wounded to the quick. The word implanted in man as the breath of God has been swamped and buried by poisonous, muddy tides of the hostile abyss. Yet the word has never been completely lost; God is mightier than the devil. In spite of the serious poisoning of the human heart, the breath that God breathes into man is by nature indestructible. God has never for a moment forsaken his work, the work that has become unfaithful to him.

Sebastian Franck continues: Christ steps in at this God-ordained point. As the new word of love,

Gen. 3:1–6

1 Tim. 2:5

Christ raises the old word of the first creation out
of the mud of the hostile forces that had buried it.
Thus new birth from God becomes possible. Thus
the deeply hidden image of God comes to light again.
Like a spark from stone, it is coaxed out of hearts that
have grown cold. The kindling word that is Christ
falls from God with its bright new fire into the sparks
of the old creation, which were threatening to die
out under the smothering ashes, and makes radiant
flames flare up again.

Through the new, the old is roused to new life
insofar as it was truly of God as the first creation:
the new word of the final revelation is stronger than
the old word of the first creation. The greater deed is
that the new Christ sets human nature free from the
self-will, self-chosen power, and possessions that have
buried it since time immemorial. What had slipped
almost completely out of God's hands is brought back
through Christ to unclouded community with God!
Now, however, everything that had to do with self is
buried in Christ; everything that unites is risen in
Christ. The word begins its work with mighty results.
The light of the indwelling Christ, as his living,
powerful word, rules in the newly born heart: God's
kingdom breaks in. The kingdom of man collapses.

It is a question of God. What matters is his
word – his first word at the beginning of creation, his
prophetic word given to people's inmost hearts, the
word that became flesh in the historical Jesus, the
renewing word of the Spirit of the indwelling Christ
(the end of all human works and interpretations),
and the recognition of God's word in Jesus Christ
as the sole authority – all this is what matters, and   Phil. 2:10–11

quite especially for a real understanding of the holy
scriptures!

Nature is not God

It is true that Sebastian Franck stood very clearly
and definitely for the Apostolic Confession of Faith
with all its articles and for the indispensability of
the Ten Commandments. But even into this very
positive train of thought there creeps the grievous
distress of his own struggles. His mystical thinking
leads to unbearable inner tension when he confronts
his principles of faith, just as he does all passages of
scripture, with the most violent contradictions. As
with the word of the scriptures, which is hidden from
all human understanding, he imagines that he can
testify to the incomprehensible God himself only
when he allows the most contradictory ideas about
God to come up with full force against each other.

The divine word must seem foolish to all people.
All human judgment is and remains disputable, a
matter of conflicting opinions. We can never swear
by our human knowledge. The very fact of these contradictions should make it clear to us that faith can
be implanted only as a cross; it can never be learned.
Sebastian Franck says that the seeker, in anxious fear
and need, must be driven to the scriptures, then away
from the scriptures, and then back to the scriptures
once more. Those who are astray must be driven
even more astray. They must be reduced to formless chaos if they want to come under God's word
and Spirit. If God is to come to them, they must be
shocked and horrified.

God separates himself sharply from the whole
world and from all flesh; the cleft seems unbridgeable.

But then in this same Sebastian Franck we find tenets
of faith that were bound to estrange him not only
from Wittenberg and Rome, Zurich and Geneva,[29] but
also from Schwenckfeld and the group named after
him: he believed that the seeds of spiritual things, the
things of God, are inborn in our hearts in the same
way as the five natural senses. He says that ultimately
the divine seed of the implanted word is identical
with the light of nature, which even the heathen recognize; Socrates – who was repeatedly compared with
Jesus by Sebastian Franck – was, like other pagans,
directly spoken to by the living voice and the blowing
Spirit of God; the nature of God is at all times and all
places the same – unity.

At one point Sebastian Franck says that God alone
is the mover of all things and all creatures, that he
loved us first of all and sought us out, he wooed
and courted us in the first place, he pursued us (his
enemies) before we wanted to know anything about
him. In another place he says that God is in himself
immovable, without will and without person until
he becomes in us, and only in us, a will that can
be moved. In some passages he testifies that God
can indeed do everything, but he does not choose
to do everything: he never chooses to do wrong,
he never chooses what is contrary to justice and
loving-kindness; what he wants to do, he does, but his
wanting is only under one condition – Christ. Yet in
other passages he seems to do away with all distinc-
tions between God and nature insofar as the latter is
still the pure creation of his divine word.

---

29 Reference to followers of Martin Luther in Wittenberg, of the pope in
    Rome, of Ulrich Zwingli in Zurich, and of John Calvin in Geneva.

In the face of all these contradictions, the brotherhood movement known as Hutterian held the living
word to be always in perfect unison with the witness
of the Bible. For this reason, its members could not
mention Sebastian Franck among their teachers of
truth although they adopted several objectively true
teachings from him, as they did from similarly moved
men of Reformation times. This movement, fighting
in visible unity and vigorous mission work for the
eternal truth of the church (the truth of the living
word) was in intimate contact with all streams of that
exceedingly moved and inspired Reformation period.
And yet it never absorbed anything but the pure truth
of God in Jesus Christ, that truth which through the
Holy Spirit is always at one with the word of the Bible.

This fact is seen at its clearest in the case of
Thomas Müntzer (the most singular man of this
mighty age) and verified by the old but still largely
unpublished teachings of the Hutterian brothers.[30] In
several unjustified suspicions, Thomas Müntzer was
defended by the brothers, but they never went along
with the erroneous and impossible alliance between
the hammer of the word and the sword of bloody
insurrection.

The word and a sword for the poor[31]

Thomas Müntzer (ca. 1489–1525) was not only an
enemy of the authorities; he was an enemy of that

---

30 The Hutterites have preserved several hundred sermons from the
sixteenth and seventeenth centuries. Arnold collected many of these on
his trip to America in 1930 and 1931.

31 Eberhard Arnold never finished this book. The remainder was compiled
posthumously by his son Eberhard C. H. Arnold. Following his father's
suggestions, he based the following section on a series of talks Eberhard
Arnold held in October 1933 on Müntzer, using Otto H. Brandt's
Thomas Müntzer: Sein Leben und seine Schriften (Eugen Diederichs
Verlag, 1933).

gospel which uplifts and edifies all without offending
anyone – the gospel the princes loved so well, the
approach so convenient for the rich. He did not want
the word of God to become petrified in the Bible. He
believed that the word of God sounds through all ages
in a living way. As people become open to it, they hear
it as God's voice in their hearts. The idea of conquest
and violence was by no means the main thing in
Thomas Müntzer's militant attitude to life. On the
contrary, he wanted us to read from God's lips, to hear
from the mouth of God himself. The saying of Jesus,
"Man does not live by bread alone but by every word
that proceeds out of the mouth of God," Müntzer
interpreted in this way: here you can see that the
word does not come from books but directly from the
mouth of God. He wanted to proclaim the faith that
would also change the outward form of government.

Matt. 4:4

When faith comes to us, it is essential that through
Christ's becoming man we become God's pupils,
that we are now taught by God himself, and that our
earthly life falls into line with the life of the heavenly
kingdom. Thus each person has to learn the artistry
of God, the forceful word of the Father, through being
illumined by the Holy Spirit. We have to be filled
with the Holy Spirit in the length, breadth, depth,
and height of our souls. Through the Holy Spirit, we
must learn to suffer the working of God; the sun must
rise in our hearts from its true place of origin. But of
course, any who have not first suffered through the
night will not experience the rising of the sun of the
rightful word. We must be so completely ready for
our own nature to be put to death that "our name
is made to stink spiritually among the godless," and

only then may we preach God's name. Christ must preach in our hearts first; only then can we give a witness to his word. God's hand must first bring us to humility before him; otherwise we are unable to recognize the truth. We must be taught by Christ himself. We must go to the original source so that fire is sent into our hearts and consciences. Then the word of God will enlighten us; the Spirit will explain the truth to us and transfigure it in such a way that we are ready to give our lives for it. We must call to God in prayer until he reveals himself and is ready to show himself to our hearts and reveal his word. Then we must give witness to this innermost revelation of the divine. Only in this way can we understand the holy scriptures.

Even under torture, Thomas Müntzer declared that worst of all was, as the common people said, that God's word was not rightly preached to them. Where freedom of the word is forbidden, we have to do everything to bring it back, for we should not allow ourselves to be restricted in or diverted from this freedom. The teaching of the Spirit and his word has to be so single, undivided, and so universally understandable that the demands made by God and Jesus Christ can be grasped by the humblest or the lowliest. The uniting spark must leap past the letter, past all human erudition, to reach and kindle even the simplest of hearts.

God wants to speak his holy word in our hearts, but we will not be able to hear it until we have an insight into our own innermost hearts. First of all, after we have conquered our fear, we must be ready to crucify completely all our desires, all our urge for ownership, and all our covetous urge for possession,

otherwise the field of life stays full of thorns and this-
tles. Before the seed of the living word can enter into
us, the plowshare must break up the field and root
out the weeds. Without this new plowing and turning
over from rock bottom up, no one can be a Christian.
No one can become sensitive to God's work and
God's word without this revolution of one's feelings,
ways of thinking, and will. The pious want nothing to
do with all this because they reject the "bitter Christ,"
"they gorge themselves to death on the honey of their
sickly-sweet piety."[32] They lack the whole Christ
because they have lost the bitter cross. The teaching
of the bitter Christ, the witness of the completely
revolutionary cross of Christ in all its seriousness, is
in sharp contrast to the imaginary faith held by the
general run of the pious. Only when the Holy Spirit
speaks into the depths of a purified and freed spirit
can the bitter Christ be revealed as the redeemer.
"The lying fabrications of false Christianity must be
torn up so that the true and authoritative epistle of
Christ can take its place."

From the Harz Mountains, addressing the miners
of Mansfeld, Thomas Müntzer declared:

> It is impossible to say anything to you in God's name
> as long as these tyrants rule over you. The oppression
> is so great that the poor are no longer capable of
> reading those things that might move their hearts
> and make them glad. And then the false prophets
> come along and preach in the most shameless way
> from their pulpits that the poor should continue to
> let themselves be worked to the bone by the tyrants;
> for that, they say, is the right way of Christ, to be

---

32 Brandt, *Thomas Müntzer*, 139.

made humble. When should the poor read the scriptures, then? When should they come to a recognition of the truth? When will the false prophets tell the rich and the princes to divest themselves of all their power and riches and humble themselves? And when will they tell them that they are not going the way of Christ, because they keep aloof from poverty and degradation?[33]

We must be empty to receive Christ

If Thomas Müntzer is, therefore, a bitter enemy of the economic and political tyrants, his enmity springs from opposition to that meta-physical, meta-political, meta-economic, and superhuman tyrant, the devil. The most thorough liberation from the ultimate tyranny is liberation from the power of the devil. We become free from this power only when we wait with eager, expectant hearts for the living word of God, the liberating word of Christ, with which Jesus put Satan to flight. We need outward freedom in order to gain inner freedom; we need stillness for God, room for his liberating inner word.

We must become quite empty before God in Christ can enter into us through the Holy Spirit. Stripped of all comfort and pride, we must lie prostrate at God's feet before God can come to lead us, the dead and the slain, to resurrection. An utter agony of despair must knock at the doors of our hearts – only then are we allowed to hear about faith. Those who dare to speak about faith in any other circumstances have stolen it; they preach what has never been tested in themselves. In truth, they are completely devoid of faith and love;

---

33 Brandt, *Thomas Müntzer*, 75.

they even hinder the working of the Holy Spirit with their vain talking. Everything they preach about faith and love is stolen goods, which can go to no one's heart. Therefore, instead of preaching empty words and dead Christianity to people, our aim must be to bring them first of all to ignorance. They shall no longer know anything, no longer be capable of anything, so that they can now be taught by the Holy Spirit himself, the Spirit of truth.

The false prophets of today want us to burst suddenly into faith; they do not want the experience of fighting their way through disbelief and despair. But anyone who refuses to go through this experience really knows absolutely nothing about faith. "He is nothing but a treacherous scribe, who uses the stolen scriptures for his own honor and glory." He knows nothing of what God himself says to people. He gladly accepts the written word itself, but he will not accept the One who inspired it. Those who have never had faith without any faith, hoped against all hope, loved against all love, know nothing of God. They have not yet seen the lamb, who alone has the power to open the book. Faith begins only when the word becomes Rev. 5 flesh in us, when Christ is born in us, when we are transplanted from Adam into Christ, when we are reborn, and when the love of God is poured into our hearts. The word that is merely heard and read kills; it never gives life: "Reading and hearing alone is ape-like mimicry; to accept the outward scripture is to feast and drink at Christ's expense; just as the most cunning thieves manage to steal the best books, faith in the Bible is like the empty faith of rogues and scoundrels." All this hinders Christ from coming.

It is a lie to say that the scriptures take the first place. No, they never take the first place, but they make a valuable witness on the way. As a witness they have real importance. We need to become completely ignorant, completely broken and humble, and only so shall we come to the point where we can give witness that Christ has become flesh. "All popes and tyrants, whether in Rome or Wittenberg,[34] must be overthrown, for it is they who cannot understand Christ because they themselves want to be preachers of the gospel. They are puppet popes, who cannot change for the good because they preach for their own glory with heart and soul, flesh and blood, bone and marrow." Those who are gripped by Christ, however, must follow in Christ's footsteps; and no commentary on the Bible or manmade glossary of the holy scriptures is a help. All these defenses of human faith can only be a hindrance.

The Son of God has said, "The scripture gives witness." The scribes say, "The scripture gives faith." Witness it can give, but never faith. It can be a help or a service – therefore it should be read and proclaimed – but it can never itself be the cause of faith. In an interpretation of Psalm 19, addressed to one of his best pupils, Thomas Müntzer says that the word of God must be taught afresh prophetically, not according to an outward understanding of the word, but rather from the living voice that comes down to us from heaven; we must understand everything with our eyes fixed on the dawn of Christ. After the long night, the sun must rise out of its true origin – God. We must first of all know that we are in the night,

---

34 Müntzer refers to Martin Luther.

and then after this night the true word will be shown
abroad in full daylight, and the beloved bridegroom
will come from his chamber like a strong man. But
for the person who has not gone through the night,
the sun of the true word will not shine. It is essential
to make a sharp distinction between this inner word
of our beloved Christ and the outward scripture. The
latter is a pointer, an interpretation, and instantiation,
or a witness to the innermost treasure; it is an instrument. But then the Master must step in, for he alone
can give the melody, impart the substantive content.
Therefore you must not take one passage from one
place in the Bible and another from another place, out
of context. Rather, you must grasp the whole spirit
of the scriptures, zealously comparing passages with
each other, which is possible only with the help and
enlightenment of the Holy Spirit.

> Therefore, in truth, no scholar understands the holy
> writ. The universities are the greatest confusers of
> the word of the Bible and always will be to the end
> of days. They give all kinds of meanings to outward
> things, but they do not recognize the essential
> meaning. Nothing will be disclosed to them because
> they do not yet walk in the Spirit; they cannot come
> to faith because they are still rich in their own spirit;
> they are not yet shrouded in the deepest darkness,
> therefore the nightingale of the Holy Spirit does not
> sing for them. They lack the inner word in the depths
> of their souls because they imagine they already have
> enough in big books. They lack the true word, on
> which the Holy Spirit depends, because at the bottom
> of their hearts is nothing but scholarship of the letter.
> They want to conjure the Spirit out of the letter of

the scriptures, like magicians telling fortunes with cards. They want to make the true dawn of the new day arise out of tattered pages. They want to place the outward testimony above Christ. They are not even as far as Moses, for Moses was conscious of the strength of God in the depths of his soul. They think they can teach faith with human theology, and they have not yet realized that faith can be given only in the cross of utter poverty of spirit. For them, dawn cannot break because they deny the night: the day cannot dawn in their hearts because in the midst of night they imagine themselves already in the day.

Bible scholars say that the written word is the voice of Christ. They take the birdcage for the bird, but the bird is no longer inside. They put a music box in the birdcage to make sounds like a bird, but with that, the living bird is by no means there. They make a trumpet of the letter, but they cannot blow it because the right sound is not in it. The right sound has to be added to it, otherwise the trumpet must be thrown away. [35]

We understand the Bible through discipleship

The Bible is not to be understood grammatically but through an inner maturing, through discipleship of Christ, through going the way of the Holy Spirit and being so filled with the Spirit that we are sure of God. This way is extremely dangerous, but it is the only way: here is an interpretation of all sayings, leading to the highest order; an explanation of ecstasy; an interpretation of the innermost word, unlocking its divine treasure; the omnipresence of God, granted as actual

---

35 Brandt, *Thomas Müntzer*, 145–146.

experience; the lightning that puts all that is indi-
vidual and isolated into the context of the whole; and
the fountainhead of the thoughts of the Holy Spirit,
illuminating the whole Bible. On this way, quite
spontaneously, a complete letting-go of everything, a
supreme yielding to God, wells up like a spring.

Therefore it is on this way that the inner word is
given. Here free will is given, wholeheartedly devoted
to listening to the voice of God. Here purity is
revealed, the strength of love is granted, and the fact
of unity is given. The way begins anew, and the spark
is kindled, the light is lit, and those things that God
does not want to withhold are boldly and passionately
called for. On this way the free will presses vigorously
on. We want to assure ourselves of the innermost
word; we look completely into the future and yet have
the future in the present. The word is no longer far
away – it is in our hearts. The heavenly voice is quite
near, not even as far away as the preacher from those
to whom he preaches. The voice is quite near to you,
so near that it is entirely within you; and therefore
on this way is faith. What no one is able to perceive
from without or experience from within is given as a
revelation – how good God is, how he loves to speak
to each one who will truly listen to him.

Deut. 30:11–14

Only those, then, who have a revelation from God
may speak of the word of God. There has always
been this revelation. The wise men of the East had
heard the word speaking within them and had seen it
shining above them; and so they came to the Christ
who, although he was still to be born, was already
born in their hearts. Things become known that
are to come to this world in the blowing wind of the

Matt. 2:1–2

coming kingdom of God; they are given to believers in the present through the constant speaking of the Spirit. When Jesus said "My words will not pass away," he was not speaking of the print in books, for that is not at all important: it is only a product of this nature and this creation. He meant that those words spoken by him as Mary's son on the way to the cross, to the resurrection, and to his ascension will be spoken in the hearts of believers everywhere and at all times through the Holy Spirit. Therefore we may not say with the false prophets: Jesus said that, for it is written in the Bible. Rather, we have to say with the true prophets: This is what the Lord says; he says it at the present time in what is new, in what is now and in the present tense. With God, nothing is in the past; everything is present. The revelation that goes on in the church is the revelation of this inner word. God is always ready to speak to us.

Matt. 24:35

Everyone can read the scripture, the word, that is in his or her heart, and yet Christ is never born in a covetous heart of any kind, as Thomas Müntzer says. God speaks his holy word into the inmost recesses of the soul and directs the despairing soul to new birth. Our inmost heart is like the document on which God's finger inscribes his immovable will and eternal wisdom. The word begins to dawn on the conscience, is spoken into the soul, and is given existence by being born. What is then born is not just anything – general, indefinite, or incomprehensible – but the King of the Jews, who was crucified under Pontius Pilate, Jesus Christ, the son of Mary. He reveals his fullness in the depths of the human soul; in the coming kingdom, he will lead in the rulership of God over all the earth.

The living word unites the church

It is astonishing that long after almost everyone else had broken with Thomas Müntzer, the brothers who are called Hutterian continued in their writings to acknowledge the truth entrusted to him. The reason was that this peasant leader was given a light that was extremely powerful. It is a terrifying thing that someone who was given so much light could commit the grave historical mistake of leading the oppressed and rebellious masses in violent revolt. We can be all the more thankful for the indescribable grace given by God to the brotherhood named after Jakob Hutter: that all this light, all this clarity, was further deepened and purified there, also from violent participation in politics and rebellion. The word of Jesus Christ and the truth the prophets and apostles represented from the beginning can only truly come into its rightful authority when it is carried out in a life that has been renewed, a life in common, filled and guided by the fire of the Holy Spirit and the fiery light of the living word.

When the word of God was given to the German-speaking lands in Reformation times, it meant two things: first, the rediscovery of the Bible in all its breadth and depth, in its integrity and clarity; second, the coming of the word of God as God's voice speaking in the hearts of believers through the Holy Spirit. In this relationship between the word of God in the heart and the word of God in the Bible, in this coming of the word of God, the life-giving Spirit is decisive. The living Christ himself is in this Holy Spirit, whom we can receive in no other way than through becoming one with the crucified Christ. This is the way God's truth is revealed.

Thus the holy scripture lying in front of us on the table is opened up to us only when simultaneously the revelation of the Holy Spirit begins to speak the inner word in our hearts. And precisely through this, the Bible that is physically present comes to life and becomes truly clear in every way. The unity of the church of the Spirit lets us see the early Christian times in the written Bible, lets us hear the living word of God directly from the mouth of God through his Holy Spirit. This faith by revelation as a recognition of the truth goes hand in hand with the holy scriptures. This, then, is the unity of the apostolic church: taking hold of the perfect unity of the kingdom of God through the living word and at the same time recognizing this word in the Bible, as it was once given directly to the prophets and to the apostles.

The church of Jesus Christ must be constantly built up anew through the word of God. She must be kept from going astray through the word of God; she must recognize error and must receive into her heart the pure wisdom of the living seed, that is to say, the direct word of God given through the Holy Spirit. Col. 3:16 The church of Jesus Christ expects this revelation daily. What the Spirit says directly to the open and Rev. 3:6 expectant church cannot be said by any human. The divine will is made known to her by God himself. When that really and truly takes place, we are completely at one with the Bible of the prophets and the apostles. Everything the Spirit says to the church now has long been put into words by the holy scriptures, only it is hidden between the covers of the Bible and inaccessible until we are taught directly by the Holy Spirit. We must let ourselves be instructed by him

in all the things asked of us, but we can do that only
when we receive the Spirit of Christ.

The word will show its power in deeds

If God did not speak again and again, he would be
a dumb god, a dead god. We believers must consult
the mouth of God constantly. Any insight grasped
through the Holy Spirit is absolutely one with the
holy scriptures. Christ is one with the Spirit. Being
Master of the word, he gives the key to the written
and printed word. We must become conscious of the
word, ready to receive it through a movement of the
Holy Spirit in our hearts. God speaks in our hearts
and points through the Holy Spirit to the work of God.

Whoever does not know the Holy Spirit is blind,
no matter how often he may read the Bible. When
God himself speaks his holy word into the depths
of our hearts, its working will emerge in deeds and
works that in everything are God's works alone. That
can only happen when we have become a dwelling
place for God and his Holy Spirit, so that more and
more – in our whole life – God's witness is turned into
works and deeds. Then the whole of life will represent what God imparts directly to our hearts through
his living word. It emerges from the innermost   John 14:23
recesses of our hearts and becomes a visible reality
in life. (If that does not happen, then what arises
within us does not come from the Holy Spirit.) The
picture such a life presents, however, will very clearly
and definitely agree in every detail with the whole
of the Bible and with all the words of Christ. In this
way, everything the Holy Spirit reveals and proclaims
in our hearts will be resolutely put into practice as

God's work and not ours. God's works proclaim the power of his word.

Acts 2:41-47 Those who have been taught by the Holy Spirit and have accepted the living word into their hearts agree with one another in utmost harmony. They are united – in all the words the Spirit has spoken – with all those who are likewise called, with the whole clear history of the apostles and the messengers of God, and with all the prophets. They are at one with the whole testimony of truth in the holy scriptures and all words of faith, for the Spirit of God has come into their hearts. Therefore our attitude toward holy scripture should be such that the Bible determines which spirits belong to God, and which to the devil. When the verdict of the Holy Spirit breaks through in us, when the movement of the Holy Spirit stirs within us, then we become at one with the entirety of holy scripture.

In the same way that any work requires suitable tools and materials, the Spirit of Christ uses the word of the apostles and prophets as his instrument. He had filled the prophets and apostles and their words – as their Spirit, he wants to fill us also. In our spirit he reminds us of all the sayings we find in the Gospels. Through our conscience he urges us to deepen our knowledge and acceptance of the word through constant reading and listening. In our heart he transforms the inwardly comprehended word of the gospel into a living expression of his nature. Just as the living word testifies to the powerful influence of Christ's presence, the Spirit of Christ turns the written or printed letters into an expression of his very being, coming directly from Christ himself.

Therefore when our lives have been renewed through a common faith in Christ, we do not demand the appearance of Christ's body, as if it were necessary to bring Christ down from heaven or even up from the kingdom of the dead. Rather, we experience the living presence of Christ's Spirit through the word that has directly pierced our hearts. The life-giving word, as the fullest expression of the experience of our hearts, is spoken out and confessed with our mouths. Faith in Jesus Christ and the confessing of his name are alive as soon as the word, like a living seed, is planted directly into our innermost hearts. When the word is near, it means that God is near. For the word is Jesus Christ himself; out of his Spirit is born every sentence of the truth.

Rom. 10:6–8

We live by every word from the mouth of God

From the beginning, Jesus Christ has been the revelation of the Father, which reached its culmination in history when he became flesh and dwelt among us. His life brought the word among us as the will of God put into practice in actual life. Therefore, in the word, Luther saw life and blessedness, forgiveness and the sharing of a common life in God. The keeping of the word can be no blind, outward obedience such as a soldier pays to military orders. It is unity of life with Jesus Christ, the Lord and bridegroom of the soul, energetically being put into practice here and now.

There is no other way of bringing forth life than through the living and abiding word of truth. If God's word is not in us, we directly oppose life and truth: we belong to death and lies. When our being is truly renewed, our strength is that we live from every word that proceeds from the mouth of God. Our inner life will be strong and victorious to the same degree that we make this triumphant saying a reality: our life owes its existence and its strength to every word of God.

It is a most remarkable inner experience to recognize more and more deeply that the Lord is alive and at work in the whole word. As long as we suppress parts of his scriptures, push them aside, or just refuse to acknowledge them, our inner life will suffer a heavy loss because we withdraw it from the full and undiminished light of the Lord himself. If we are unable to see how to apply some part of the Bible to our life because it has not yet become important to us, we should remember in what way God's life came into our hearts. What we to our joy and delight have experienced from Christ as an inner word used to be mere letters, cold and alien to us.

Out of the unfathomable depths of the word (which are perhaps still remote to us), the Spirit wants to let undreamed-of aspects of the living reality of God and Christ sink into our hearts. If we try to avoid God's working in any area, no one can tell how much we have forfeited in life. Every word of the Lord in his scriptures is meant to become our inner experience and possession through the Holy Spirit. What Jesus said in a very serious hour is one of life's deepest truths: "Man lives by every word that proceeds out of the mouth of God." The closer we come to the goal most important for our inner life – that the whole of the written word comes alive in us – the stronger, holier, and more powerful will our life be.

Matt. 4:4

How far are we on the way to this goal? The

answer depends most of all on how deeply the word has taken root in our inner being, how much we treasure it in our heart. Whoever receives the word with joy and tries to have faith for a time, but falls away again and loses everything in a moment of temptation, has in fact gained nothing. The hours of temptation test whether or not the word has been deeply planted in us and has taken root. "As for what was sown on good soil, this is the man who after he has heard the word cherishes it in a good and upright heart." Only those who cherish the word and keep it belong to God; they love him, and in them the Father and the Son make their dwelling.

Luke 8:11–28

Love and loyalty to the word are determined through the innermost direction of the will. Teresa rightly describes love as the arrow shot by the will.[36] In his word, God makes known his will, which is love. He lets the truths of this word pierce our hearts as the sharp arrows of his love. In the same way, only a firm and taut-strung will is capable of sending our love toward God's heart and of showing the same love to all people by carrying out his word faithfully, using love's weapons. Only when our soul has a firm and decided will can it recognize the word of Jesus as the true issuing-forth of God's nature: "If someone wants to do the will of him who sent me, he will know whether this teaching is from God." The energy for all acts of obedience is born out of a common inner will with God, in which the heart says to God, "What will you have me do?"

John 7:17

For this reason, all powerful expression of inner life depends on one condition: whether the word of

---

36 Teresa of Ávila, 1515–1582, Spanish mystic and Carmelite nun.

God is alive in us. Only those in whom God's words abide are promised that everything they ask will

1 John 5:15 be granted them. The living word within them is the leading of the Spirit in their deeds and in their prayers. The firm word of God in their hearts is the rock foundation on which they feel secure. It fills their hearts with certainty: they have the fulfillment of their prayers before anyone else can see it.

Without the living word within us, we cannot be certain that our prayers will be answered or that evil will be overcome. Through the sword of the word, the

Matt. 4:7, 10 Lord vanquished the tempter. Scripture also tells us that the disciples were strong and had overcome evil because the word of God dwelt in them. There is no victory over sin unless the word is cherished in the inmost depths of our hearts, as the Old Testament

Ps. 119:11 singer says: "I have kept your word in my heart so that I do not sin against you!" There is only one way of abiding in the Father and in the Son: letting the word

1 John 2:24 we have heard from the beginning abide in us.

The written word (which must be a dead letter to unbelief) becomes so alive in a believing heart that at every crossroad and in every danger it is ready to be

Ps. 119:104–105 our unerring guide. Through his word, Jesus comes to meet us as our Lord. His authority to lead us and to direct our lives in all things is felt in our innermost hearts to be his holy right, and to obey it is our highest calling.

In the German Youth Movement, the ideal of a born leader was glorified – the picture of a personality full of greatness and beauty, full of love and authority, full of spirit and strength. Above all, it was emphasized that leading was an inner vocation, which no one can be given from without; the true leader is not chosen but appears among his people and chooses them. He is a man of strong will and high purpose.

Only Jesus is this real leader who in truth and purity fulfills the longing of youth and of all deeply thinking people. Spirit and love are united in him in one personality. It was Jesus who came up to his people and called out with free and perfect authority, "Follow me!" "Whoever does not leave everything and follow me is not worthy of me." Today it is through his word, bringing his presence near, that he sends the same call of discipleship to his chosen. For the word is his personal will, through which he shows himself as a leader; his authority overpowers all those who hear his call and wins them for himself. Discipleship won in this way through a complete inner uniting differs sharply from being submerged in a vague principle, in a power of love that rules the universe. For with discipleship, it is a question of the most personal of personal relationships. It is a question of an absolute relationship to an unexampled human life, which, through his word, stands clearly and uniquely outlined before us.

Mark 2:14

Matt. 10:37–38

Acts 17:11

The living word is a trustworthy guide [37]
Being led inwardly through God's word can never be replaced by an imitation. There are people in mountainous districts who want to manage without a guide. They are the notorious stragglers who, always at a safe distance, try to follow others who have a guide. When we hear of a serious accident in the mountains, the first question is always whether the

---

37 This conclusion is taken from the 1923 edition of *Innenland*, with Arnold's own revisions.

victims had been without a guide, trying to imitate
others who were being quite safely led. No one is able
to manage without a personal guide in the dangerous regions through which the narrow way leads us.
Whoever has ventured into the rugged mountains of
life without the clear inner leading of the word goes
to meet a terrible disaster, no matter how much he
keeps the example of other people in view – people
who really are being led.

When the Lord gives us inner guidance, it often
happens that in each situation the right scriptural
word is given – indeed, a radiant light is poured over
whole passages of scripture for our inner growth.
This helps us to understand why Tersteegen[38] had
to conclude that when God's light showed him the
meaning of a word of scripture for his personal
renewal, strengthening, and guidance, it was each
time the actual meaning of this word. Therefore, what
is important for him is the strength of the impact
when the Spirit and meaning of the word strike our
hearts to meet our need. Committing a passage to
memory word for word or according to logical sense
means absolutely nothing to him.

Each use of the word as mere outward form can
only darken it and alienate it from us. The letter is
not the life. But the holy scripture is a weapon to be
wielded: it is a sword of the Spirit. The Holy Spirit
alone uses the sword where and how he wills. He
must speak the word anew to each one separately.
Whereas previously (despite our intellectual knowledge of the word) we had lost all sense of direction, he
now pours the word out like a flood of light into our
hearts and upon our path. It can come upon us like an

Eph. 6:17

38 Gerhard Tersteegen, 1697–1769.

inner revelation when the word comes to life in this
way. It is like the sun suddenly breaking through the
fog to show the lost traveler his glorious path – until
then he had seen nothing but dark, ghostly shadows.

The living word at work within us directs its
far-reaching energies toward leading, mastering, and
ruling the whole of our life. True spiritual leadership
comes only through the word of God written in our
hearts and minds. This alone is sanctification of life:
if from within our hearts the will of God, completely
revealed in the word, brings our whole being to the
obedience born of faith.

Rom. 15:18

Our lives can be transformed only from within. Yet
the aim of the word alive within us is that it should be
put into practice in deeds and in truth. Only so will
it be proved that we are an epistle of Christ, written
with the Spirit of the living God on the fleshly pages
of our heart. The word of God gives us strength and
clarity in all situations and in all the demands of the
daily struggle so that we are strong and can overcome
evil. We shall be able to carry out the worldwide tasks
God has given us only when the word of God is alive
and is kept alive in us.

2 Cor. 3:2–3

The word discloses the will of God to us so
that the present – uniquely significant for world
history – works toward the final goal: toward the
kingdom of God, toward the sovereign rule of Jesus
Christ. Only when people are ready to be ruled by the
will of God alone, and not by their own nature, will
the joy of true peace and genuine righteousness be
able to rule among them.

The final and complete rule of God lies still in the
future, as the horrors of our age have proved once

more. But there is an unfailing relationship between the rule of Christ in the hearts of believers and the future rule of their Lord as king. For the kingdom of God is nothing less than the will and nature of the Highest become practical reality.

The inner peace of God's rule gathers all our energies into a harmonious working-together, which the world longs for. When our inner life is ruled by the clear conviction that only in God's nature is true strength to be found, we shall make God's will a reality among people, not with new hate but with new love. When our whole life is surrendered to his lordship through the word of God, when from deep within our hearts we become alive to his will, the most sublime task will be given us, bringing the greatest joy and blessing. There is nothing greater for this earth than God's rule in the kingdom of Jesus Christ.

> Eternal Word to our hearts shown forth –
> Son of the Virgin, through the Spirit: O Lord,
> thou unitest East, West, South, and North.
> Thy new creation sings praise with one accord.
>
> Fire-glow of love and radiant light:
> bring down thy kingdom to our world of strife.
> Truth everlasting! O leave us not –
> keep us united in death, as in life. [39]

---

39 Arnold's poem, "Herzen erschlossenes ewiges Wort," *Poems and Rhymed Prayers* (Plough, 2003), 294. It was found after his death among his manuscript pages for the last chapter of this book.

Other Titles by Eberhard Arnold

God's Revolution
Justice, Community, and the Coming Kingdom
Excerpts from talks and writings on the church,
family, government, world suffering, and more.

The Early Christians
In Their Own Words
This collection of early Christian writings chal-
lenges readers to live more fully and radically.

Why We Live in Community
with two interpretive talks by Thomas Merton
A time-honored manifesto on the meaning and
purpose of community.

Salt and Light
Living the Sermon on the Mount
Thoughts on the "hard teachings" of Jesus
and their applicability today.

The Prayer God Answers
Rediscover the kind of prayer that has the power
to transform our lives and our world.

Plough Publishing House
PO BOX 398, Walden, NY 12586, USA
Robertsbridge, East Sussex TN32 5DR, UK
4188 Gwydir Highway, Elsmore, NSW 2360, Australia
845-572-3455 • info@plough.com • *www.plough.com*